The Salt Block

The Salt Block

✦

*Heartwarming Stories
from a Cowboy-Pastor*

By Bubba Stahl

Bubba Stahl

Psalm 86:11-13

iUniverse, Inc.
New York Lincoln Shanghai

The Salt Block
Heartwarming Stories from a Cowboy-Pastor

iUniverse books may be ordered through booksellers or by contacting:

iUniverse
2021 Pine Lake Road, Suite 100
Lincoln, NE 68512
www.iuniverse.com
1-800-Authors (1-800-288-4677)

Because of the dynamic nature of the Internet, any Web addresses or links contained in this book may have changed since publication and may no longer be valid.

The views expressed in this work are solely those of the author and do not necessarily reflect the views of the publisher, and the publisher hereby disclaims any responsibility for them.

Scripture quotations are from The Holy Bible, English Standard Version, copyright ã 2001 by Crossway Bibles, a publishing ministry of Good News Publishers.

ISBN: 978-0-595-46627-6 (pbk)
ISBN: 978-0-595-70948-9 (cloth)
ISBN: 978-0-595-90922-3 (ebk)

Printed in the United States of America

This book is dedicated to my beautiful wife, Beth Stahl, and to our sons and their families; Ben and Kelly and their children Camille, Emma, Charlie, and Olivia; Dan and Chana' and their daughter, Chandler.

"For I know the plans I have for you, declares the LORD, plans for wholeness and not for evil, to give you a future and a hope." Jeremiah 29:11

"Therefore, since we are surrounded by so great a cloud of witnesses, let us also lay aside every weight, and sin which clings so closely, and let us run with endurance the race that is set before us, looking unto Jesus, the founder and perfecter of our faith, who for the joy that was set before him endured the cross, despising the shame, and is seated at the right hand of the throne of God."
Hebrews 12:1-2

Contents

Acknowledgements

Many people have encouraged me over the years to write down these stories. I want to thank my sister, Debbie Livingston, for reading the first manuscript and helping me with grammar, punctuation, and overall style. She is a high school teacher and knows books as well as anyone I know. I also want to thank a good friend and church member at First Baptist Church in Corpus Christi, Dr. Shirley Peddy. She has written several books and teaches at Del Mar College in Corpus Christi. Shirley proofread the first and second manuscripts and gave experienced suggestions and corrections. I also want to thank Ardis Click and Aida Guzman for proofreading during the editing stages. Thank you Debbie, Shirley, Ardis, and Aida for overlooking my cowboy English and grammar.

I also handed out a trial run of this book to several members of the First Baptist Church in Corpus Christi and received much encouragement. Of course, the people of the First Baptist Church are all encouragers.

Most of all, I want to thank my wife, Beth Stahl. She read and corrected, read and corrected, read and reread this manuscript and has supported me from the very beginning. Her faithfulness to Christ and to His church is a constant source of encouragement to me and to many, many others.

Bubba Stahl
May, 2007

Introduction

God called me into the ministry in 1982. Before that I was a cowboy. Since then God has allowed us to pastor six different churches around the state of Texas. Over the past twenty-five years I have told many stories about cowboys and experiences from mission trips. This is a collection of some of those stories and my testimony.

A lady once told me, "You are the most low-down preacher I have ever known." She then corrected herself by saying, "What I mean is you are the most down-to-earth preacher I have ever known." It was the nicest thing anyone has ever told me.

The Good News of Jesus Christ is "low-down." Jesus came down to our level, a very low-down condition. He spoke our language and told us very clearly how much God loved us. He provided for us a new relationship with God and He gave us hope. Jesus Christ is our hope. He is God's love for us, now and forever. We do not have to wait until forever to experience eternal life. We can have abundant life now by receiving Jesus Christ and have a new relationship with God in Him.

Each of these stories points out something about the Lord and the abundant life He gives. All of the stories are from my own experiences. I have tried to arrange these stories in chronological order.

My wife, Beth, saw many of these stories first hand and was the first one to hear the others. She has also heard them more times than any other person. Without her encouragement and inspiration there would only be cowboy stories because she is the one who believed when I didn't and stayed with it when I wanted to give up. She has made a home for us in old bunkhouses, church parsonages, tents, and regular houses. Each time we would move she would leave the place cleaner and better than we found it. Her faithfulness has been an anchor in all of our transitions.

I hope these stories will encourage you to see how God has worked and is working in your life. He loves us more than we know. His plan is to change us to look, sound, and be more like His Son, Jesus Christ. As we ask Him to change us, and trust what He is doing in our lives, He will change us, and our lives glorify Him.

> *"Not to us, O LORD, not to us but to your name give glory,*
> *for the sake of your steadfast love and your faithfulness."*
> Psalm 115:1[1]

My Testimony

I was born on May 16, 1953, in San Antonio, Texas. My parents had both been raised in church as their parents had, and theirs before them, so I was raised in a Christian home. The blessings of a Christian home and upbringing cannot be over emphasized. The blessings that come with being in the environment of God's Word being taught, being in the midst of God's people worshipping, and hearing all of this not only on Sunday but throughout the week at home, is the greatest thing that parents can give a child. It is more valuable than all of the education, wealth, and health benefits combined. There is no substitute for it and no one better than parents to give it.

Every Sunday morning we got up and got ready for "SundaySchool-andChurch." My computer does not recognize that word but it was one word around the Stahl house. I would hear my mother, Louise Stahl, whistling hymns like "Blessed Assurance" and "Standing On The Promises." My dad, Dick Stahl, would come in our rooms every Sunday morning and give us our allowance, ten dimes. He taught us early that ten percent was to be given to God with gratitude, ten percent was to be put in our piggy bank as savings, ten percent was to be put in our pockets for spending money, and we were to use seventy percent to pay our bills with. We did not know what that meant at the time, but daddy simply explained that we would know later and for the moment it meant more spending money. We would get all dressed up in our Sunday clothes, fill out our envelopes, get our Bibles and Sunday

School books and head out to church. This was our weekly routine. On Wednesdays we went to prayer meeting.

There was never any questioning whether we were going to church: we just did. And if we squirmed around too much or complained about how long the service was we got into trouble, not in the church, but outside or when we got home. At church we would get "the look." From mama, the look was squinted eyes; from daddy, it was widening eyes, which was far more serious than the squinted eyes. Either look, it was not a good thing at all to act up at church. We did not realize at the time, of course, but they were teaching us respect, something that is foundational for learning anything whether it is at home, at school, or at church.

Another thing that I did not realize until much later was the blessing of not ever hearing my parents complain about the church. I never heard them say a single derogatory word about the pastor, the people, the sermon, the Sunday School teachers, the Minister of Education, the music, or the Minister of Music, never. I never asked them if they did this intentionally or not, but it taught me something very important; church was a good place no matter who was there, no matter what was happening, or not happening. It was a privilege to go to church, something to look forward to, and something you did every week.

Another thing my dad did was to teach me to sing. I knew the words to "Holy, Holy, Holy" and "The Old Rugged Cross" before I could read. He also taught me cowboy songs like "Home on the Range," "When Its Round Up Time in Texas," "Ghost Riders in the Sky," and of course, "The Eyes of Texas." I especially loved the cowboy songs because that is what I was and always wanted to be, a cowboy. Television shows like *Rawhide, Bonanza,* and *Gun Smoke* were what I lived for, and Roy Rogers was my number one hero (after daddy, of course). Hymns, Bibles, offering envelopes, Sunday School, cowboy songs, and

Roy Rogers defined my life. I do not remember the first time I went to church or heard about Jesus and His love for me. And I do not ever remember a time when I did not want to be a cowboy.

One Sunday night on the way home from church, I asked daddy again about becoming a Christian. We were members of Trinity Baptist Church in San Antonio and as a six-year-old I had been noticing many people getting baptized. We were also having the Lord's Supper a lot. This was something I was not allowed to have, which bothered me since it was a tiny piece of bread and a very small cup and seemed to be just my size, so I was asking questions about all of this.

Every time we would have the Lord's Supper, I would ask, "Now am I old enough?" and daddy would tell me that it was not about being old enough but that it was about being a Christian. He would say, "Now, Bubba, if you will be still, I will share this little bit of cracker with you and will leave a little bit of juice in the cup for you." Then he would explain to me in the faintest whisper that the broken cracker and the grape juice meant that Jesus Christ died on the cross for our sins, and we could trust Him for everything. And I would see him close his eyes in prayer.

Just before everyone would eat their cracker, he would open one eye, look at me, and break off a small flake for me. After that we would have the small cup of grape juice. I would watch him carefully, and he would leave a little more than a drop for me.

So, I was asking about becoming a Christian, and once more, daddy told me about how God sent His Son, Jesus Christ, to be the Savior for the world and how He died on the cross for all of our sins. That night, on the way home from church, as I listened again to a story that I was very familiar with, I remember thinking, "I already know how this story ends, but I will listen anyway." As daddy shared the gospel with me I remember seeing in my mind's eye a picture of Jesus on the cross, with the two thieves on either side, the Roman soldier looking up at Him, the dark sky, and sunbeams shining down on Him. As I listened to the story, looking at that picture, I realized that Jesus did not just die for "the world," *He died for me.* I do not remember praying a prayer, I just remember looking up at Jesus on that cross, like that Roman soldier was doing, and for the first time, the story was different, and it was when Jesus Christ became personal to me. I did not know much but I did believe and trust Jesus Christ as my Savior.

There have been various times in my life when I questioned my relationship with Christ, and had doubts about my salvation, and have prayed and asked myself, "When did Jesus become my personal Savior?" Every time, this is the experience I go back to because this was when I believed that Jesus died not only for the whole world, He died for me. I have prayed, asking Jesus into my heart, many times, but whenever I take the Lord's Supper, that Sunday night on the way home from church is what is clearer in my mind and heart than any thing else.

A few Sundays later I walked forward and made my decision publicly. Buckner Fanning was the pastor at that time; in fact he had just begun his long and faithful ministry at Trinity Baptist Church in San Antonio when I went forward. A few weeks later I was baptized, on Wednesday night, March 30, 1960. I know the date simply because the next day my brother, David Stahl, was born.

As I stepped down off of the last step in the baptistery, I almost got baptized. But Buckner caught me, held me up, and he said these words: "You may not be able to see this boy, but God sees him and God sees His Son in him." And with that he baptized me. I remember it well. Each time I baptize a small child, holding him up until it's time to go under, I think about what Buckner said. I pray that God will see—and that the whole world will see—His Son, Jesus Christ in us.

When I was in the third grade a man was teaching us in Sunday School. He was the first "man" teacher I remember having in Sunday School. He taught us to agree together in prayer. At the beginning of class he would ask the boys to share prayer requests. We would look around at each other not knowing exactly what to say, and then one of us would share something about how hard school was or about how the girls were bothering us. Occasionally someone would share something about a grandparent being sick. One Sunday a boy said, "my mother died last week." It got real quiet and we knew that this was a different request than usual.

No matter what the request was, this man would nod his head and then have us all take turns praying for these requests. As each boy would mention the request, our teacher would say, "Yes Lord," or "Grant it Father." He believed that God was listening to us and that every request was as important as any other request. He would agree with all of us about what we were asking God to do.

I had become a Christian and was already a cowboy. I do not remember when I became a cowboy; I just always wanted to be and I was one. I had the hat, the boots, the play guns, the stick horses, the red bandana, the whole works, and I do not remember the first ones that I had. Everything that had anything to do with the west, cowboying, horses, cows, ranches, or the country, I liked it. Daddy knew several ranchers when I was growing up. Several times a year we would go out on their ranches and help work cattle and ride horses.

When I was in junior high school, I bought my first horse. I had gone with a friend out to his ranch and the horse that I rode I learned was for sale for $150. I went home and made all of the arrangements for a place to keep him. I emptied my money jar, did a few extra yards, borrowed some, and bought him.

Old Chief was a good horse, although not very gentle. I did not have money for a saddle so I rode bareback for several months until my grandfather felt sorry for me and bought a second-hand saddle from the King Ranch Saddle Shop in Kingsville. Next to my horse, this was my most prized possession because it had the famous running W brand stamped on it. It sits today on a stand in my office at church.

When I was in junior high we did not have a youth minister, but there was a lady who took us places and taught us in training union. She was very beautiful, something we junior high boys were starting to notice. Another thing that I noticed was that her husband was confined to a wheelchair; the kind that looks more like a bed on wheels than a chair. He was paralyzed.

I asked daddy about it and learned that this young couple had committed their lives to be missionaries. While studying at the seminary, this man came down with polio and almost died. He was left paralyzed from the neck down.

They were at our church in Houston every Sunday and Wednesday just like us. She would meet the youth up at the church parking lot on Saturday evenings and take us in her car to youth rallies that were very popular back in the sixties in Houston. She had a big car that was also a convertible. I remember her driving up, getting out, and gathering up samples of various items that she was selling door to door and putting them in the trunk. I did not know what they were but knew that it was a way to make money and I wondered how she was able to take care of her husband, sell stuff, and then have the time to take us teenagers to the rallies. She was a wonderful lady.

At just about every rally I would go forward and rededicate my life to Christ. In Baptist circles this meant that you had already been saved but that you felt moved during the service to rededicate what you had already given to the Lord. Sometimes it meant that you had strayed away from the Lord and, like the prodigal son, had come back home.

After several times of going forward, the counselors asked me why I kept doing this. Was I sure that I was saved? I said yes and shared about my experience on the way home from church that Sunday night. I told them I went forward because I felt I needed to rededicate my life to the Lord.

The youth rallies were special to me because of Marion Hall, the amazing lady who took the time to help others in spite of the challenges she and her husband faced. Marion died of cancer in 1980. Her husband, Richard, lived in Carbondale, Illinois until his death in 2006. He called me one day in 1994 having heard my testimony on a tape and we became prayer partners. About three or four times a year he would call me and we would pray together. With every word I could hear the breathing machine he was on. Richard would always say, "Bubba, whenever you preach, tell the people that God loves us and in Christ we have hope and joy; now and forever!"

After high school I hustled down to Texas A&I University in Kingsville partly because my parents had gone there, partly because my grandmother and aunt and uncle lived there, and mainly because the King Ranch was there and I wanted to work on the King Ranch. I did not go there to go to school. In fact, it is really a stretch to say that I went to Texas A&I University because I did not go much. I quickly found out that I did not have to go to class like I did when I was in high school, but I did not learn until mid-semester that not going to class affected your grade. At mid-semester, grades were sent out to the address of the ones paying for the semester, in my case my parents. I was failing everything except algebra and speech class.

When I called my parents asking for more money, my dad asked me what was going on. He said, "Bubba, how do you fail P.E.? All you have to do is show up and take a shower! How can you be failing every-thing except speech and algebra?" I told him I was spending all of my time studying algebra and had not balanced it all out yet. All I had to do in speech was talk for three minutes. He was not very happy, to say the least. He told me that if I did not bring up my grades, which meant going to class, that I would flunk out and would not be able to go back. I thought that would be all right with me because all I wanted to do was to work on a ranch.

I was making good grades in algebra because that is where I met Beth Grim, in algebra class, and I was spending most of my time studying algebra with my new girlfriend. I shared my dreams of being a cowboy and some of my limited experience and Beth also had dreams of living out in the country. She was from Harlingen, Texas and had been the FFA Sweetheart, and Miss Rio Grande Valley 1970.

We spent a lot of time together that first semester, fell in love, and began making our plans for the future. On Valentine's Day, 1972, I asked Beth to marry me. I was eighteen years old, on scholastic proba-tion, looking for work on a ranch, and making plans to get married in the summer, which is just what we did. Beth and I got married on July 1, 1972. I had a job on the Braugh Ranch, located between Rivera and Falfurrias in the brush country of South Texas and had been promised a house just as soon as we got back from our honeymoon in Corpus Christi.

The house they promised was next to the bunkhouse and had been used to store hay and feed sacks. They cleaned out the hay and feed, swept it out, put new screens on the door and windows, and we moved in. It was a three-room house; a small room in the front, a bedroom, and a kitchen/bathroom. The kitchen and bathroom were really one room but were separated by a shower curtain. It had a bare concrete floor throughout the whole house; and it was in the country! That was the part that I liked the most.

Beth and I went to First Baptist Church in Kingsville even before we got married. My family, on my dad's side, had been members in that church since the 1920's. I have a picture in my office today that is dated 1926 of the members of First Baptist Kingsville with my grandmother, great-grandmother, and her mother, my great-great-grandmother in it.

After we were married Beth joined the First Baptist Church. She had been raised in the Catholic Church where her parents are very active members. They gave Beth a great respect and love for God and the Church. As a child, she wanted to be a nun, but she also wanted to have a family. Beth has shared in her testimony that God gave her both. She said being a Baptist pastor's wife is like being a "Baptist nun" and God allowed her to serve Him and have a family too.

We moved from ranch to ranch the first few years we were married. It was easy to pack up and go since we did not have many things. I was foreman of one ranch. It wasn't a very big ranch and Beth was the only ranch hand to boss around, which did not go over very well at all. If I raised my voice at all, she would quit; I'd apologize, hire her back, and we would finish feeding the cows.

Wherever we lived, we were active in the Baptist church. We ended up back in Kingsville in 1974, and I got a job on the King Ranch breaking horses and working cattle. I felt that I had reached the pinnacle of cowboy success. The only thing left for us was to own our own ranch someday, which was one of our goals in life.

We did not know how we would ever afford to buy our own place, but we knew we wanted to and had already begun to plan where everything would go, like the house, the barn, the round pen, the garden, and things like that. We had lived on enough of these ranches to know the best arrangement for such things, and we had often talked about it.

In my mind's eye I could see it as clearly as the day but did not know how we would ever have enough money to afford it. Ranch hands do not make much money and by this time Beth was pregnant with our first son, Ben. But we still dreamed and prayed that one day we would be able to have our own place.

About the time that Ben was born I was ordained as a deacon in the First Baptist Church in Kingsville. I had stopped working for the King Ranch and had begun working for the Texas Animal Health Commission. These state cowboys had come in to the King Ranch and had found fever ticks on the cattle in and around Kingsville.

Texas cattle were infested with fever ticks after the Civil War when the large cattle drives were moving to the northern markets. The Texas cattle had immunity to the disease that this particular tick carried and the northern cattle did not. By the time they discovered the problem, thousands of northern cattle had died. They learned the life cycle of this tick and started dipping the cattle in large dipping vats all over the state. The tick was finally eradicated in the U.S. and held back to the Texas/Mexico border. Mexican livestock still have the immunity that the Texas cattle once had, but the Texas cattle have lost their immunity. If the fever ticks came back in to the U.S. they could once again devastate the industry; and so the state and federal governments developed programs to protect the cattle.

The state cowboys that inspected the cattle for these ticks were cowboys but they got state pay, which was about double what ranch hands made. I had made good grades in algebra and it did not take me long to figure out that if I got a job with the state, then we could get our place quicker. So I did. I got a quick education on fever ticks and started making more money that I had ever made in my life as a livestock inspector with the state.

Working for the state of Texas was fun. I did the same cowboy work but got more pay and actually worked fewer hours. When we did work overtime, I got something that I had only heard of; overtime pay, time and a half. This was moving us closer to buying that place at a much faster pace than I had ever imagined.

Then another group came into town; federal cowboys with the United States Department of Agriculture. Guess what? They got paid about double what we state boys were getting. Again, I did the math quickly in my head and knew I had to get on with the USDA. The only thing about the federal boys was that once the Kingsville "outbreak" was under control, all of the federal boys would be sent back to the Texas/Mexico border from Del Rio to Brownsville to patrol the Rio Grande River in order to keep these fever ticks from coming across the river on Mexican livestock.

I was willing to move. Beth and I were experts at moving. We did have more stuff with Ben around, but it was not a big deal; anything in order to get more money and to buy that place of our own. The only problem was that there was a freeze on USDA hiring and so I had to wait.

So there we were in Kingsville, working for the state, cowboying and serving in just about everything up at the church. I was ordained as a deacon and would occasionally be asked to speak in church on Wednesday evenings or even during Sunday evening services. When I would share a devotional or testimony or brief "message," people would come up afterward and say, "Bubba, we think you missed your calling. You are a good preacher." I hated it when I would hear that because it made me remember when I was a teenager making all of those decisions to rededicate my life. Once I made a decision to surrender for special service, which meant you would go to seminary and be a preacher. But I loved being a cowboy and wanted to buy that place more than anything in the world. And so I would smile and say, "Thanks."

I was on the waiting list for the USDA and the state moved a bunch of us out of Kingsville to various parts of the state. I was thankful that they moved me to Falfurrias. It was a long way to drive every day, but I knew it was temporary and that shortly I would be working for the USDA.

One evening on the way back to Kingsville I became very uneasy and nervous. I kept thinking about what people said about how they were helped and encouraged whenever I would speak at church. I was doing a lot of praying and reading in my Bible, and I had always wondered about a call to the ministry. It was so strong that night that I pulled off to the side of the road and got out, walked around praying and looking up at the stars, kicked a few rocks around, got back in my truck and said to myself, "Here I am in between jobs trying to get on with the USDA, I don't know sic'em from come back about being a preacher … why in the world am I even thinking about it … what is wrong with me …?" I shook myself off, and before I knew it, I had talked myself right back into my truck with my mind set on getting on with the USDA.

A few weeks later I got that job with the USDA and started making double what I had been making with the state. I got to work back in Kingsville, on the King Ranch again. A year later we received our transfer to Eagle Pass, Texas. I had requested as far west as possible because the ranches were bigger, and it was rougher country than down in the Rio Grande Valley. I was assigned the last ride in Maverick County. Ben was eighteen months old and Beth was pregnant with Dan and we moved again.

The closest town to my ride was a place called El Indio. It was a stretch to call it a town. It had a post office, a general store, a beer joint, and a mission church. If you saw the television series *Lonesome Dove* you know what El Indio looked like; it looked like Lonesome Dove. Beth and I found a house for rent on a ranch that was about fifteen miles south of El Indio. It was the last house before an 88-mile stretch of dirt road called the Old Mines Road that ended up in Laredo, Texas. We were literally only a few miles from the end of the pavement. To say that we lived in the boondocks would be an understatement. And we loved it.

I would go out each day and ride the river, help the ranchers in the area work cattle, occasionally catch some Mexican cattle and horses, and generally had the best time of my life up to that point. I broke horses for other people because of the miles and miles of riding that was required, which was perfect for starting young horses. I also worked cattle on the side and during vacation time. Beth and I worked in the little mission church in El Indio. I played the old piano and taught the teenagers, and Beth took care of all of the small children. Dan was born while we lived in El Indio, and Ben learned to ride horses and kick cow dogs. We had it as good as it gets.

One of the ranchers that I used to help quite often came to me and asked if I would help him gather the cattle off of one of his pastures because he was going to sell the pasture. I asked him if I could buy some of it, and before I knew it, we had made a deal on five acres of land! We owned a ranch! It was a small ranch as ranches are measured, but it was ours. I fenced it and drew out a plan on a yellow pad of where the barn, round pen, house, and garden would go.

A thunderstorm and small tornado had gone through the country one night and had twisted up some old tin sheds and broken off some old telephone poles, which in El Indio are not very big—about the size of your leg. I made a deal with some of the ranchers to clean up the twisted up tin and broken boards if I could keep them. I went right to work on my barn and round pens with the scraps that I cleaned up from the storm. Right before my eyes everything had begun to take shape just as I had been planning all those years.

Beth found a used trailer house in Eagle Pass. We made a deal on it, and we had our first home, a mobile home. I put in a water line and septic tank and hauled our home out to our land. We were suddenly getting everything we had always dreamed of, our own place in the country with a nice barn, round pens, garden, flower beds, yard fence, some newly planted trees; it was nice. We had seen it all in our minds and had talked about it for so long, and yet seeing it for real was more than we had imagined. Some may not think that five acres is very much, but for us it was our own place. It did not have to be very big; it was ours and we had arranged it all just as we had dreamed it.

The barn was my living room. I had two horse pens that extended out from it with a breeze way down the middle, saddle racks on one side with my hitching post just outside, hay and feed on the other side, but handy for feeding both horses. I used to love to feed the horses in the evening and then just sit in front of them by the main middle pole in the barn and listen to them eat. There is nothing more relaxing than listening to horses eat, late in the evening, while your young cowboy sons are playing close by, with the smell of supper cooking, and the sun going down. Every day was the best day for me.

During the first part of the summer of 1982 we had a mission team from central Texas come to El Indio on a mission trip. We had seen several groups come down for mission trips and always enjoyed the company and help, but this one was different. For some reason they really got to me. Seeing these college students organize the vacation Bible school for the children and leading the services each night stirred me deeply. There were several that made decisions for Christ during that week and I was moved by it all.

About the same time, in the evenings, I would get a restless feeling while the horses were eating, and that bothered me. I had not been restless in a long time like that, and the evenings were my favorite times. It really bothered me as I sat there in my barn. I thought that I was starting to get greedy and maybe was restless because five acres was not enough; maybe I thought I needed ten. I hated greed and it bothered me that I was not content with what I had. After all, we had everything we ever wanted, and we loved it. What was wrong with me? I remember getting mad several times and just going inside before the horses were even through eating.

Another thing that was bothering me was our work at the mission. We had been serving there for a couple of years and had not seen much growth. Beth and I were doing all of the work alongside of Brother Enrique and his wife. Brother Enrique was a retired Hispanic preacher that came out to the mission every Sunday from Eagle Pass. I felt that the members, who were mostly women, needed to pick up more of the responsibilities.

I was asking God in my prayer time for "leadership and guidance" in what should be done at the mission. We had several friends at First Baptist Church in Carrizo Springs and at First Baptist Church in Eagle Pass who were praying with us. I figured that we would end up going to one of those churches soon. I had helped out in both of those churches off and on, filling in when the pastors would ask, and again hearing "You sure did miss your calling … that sure did bless me what you said …" It bothered me to hear that, but I always liked helping out.

During the summer of 1982 with the mission team from central Texas, with all my praying for "leadership and guidance" and asking God what He wanted us to do, and our friends praying for us, another strange thing happened. The Bible began to open up in ways that I had not seen before. I had always loved to read the Bible, and in high school

I carried a small New Testament with me to class and had it marked for witnessing. I didn't witness that much, but I was ready to, and I read the Bible more than anything else.

During those days of prayer that summer, the Bible came alive. Every passage I read made a lot of sense to me, and I felt that I needed to share it with somebody. I wasn't around many people at all, mostly Beth and the boys, but I was around my horses a lot, so I preached to them.

I would be horseback most of the day everyday so I would talk and preach most of the day to my horses about things that God was show-ing me in the Bible. As I did, I would see in my mind's eye myself preaching to crowds of people, which I thought was pretty funny since we lived way out, and I was really very nervous around people. I have always preferred to be by myself. It wasn't that I did not like people; I was just shy and nervous around people and got tired quickly around them. I have often wondered if my old horses thought that I had lost my ever-loving mind the way I had started getting so talkative all of a sudden. It didn't seem to bother them any, and it helped me to get some of these messages talked out.

On August 7, 1982 I had an experience with the Lord. It was on a Saturday and Beth had gone into Eagle Pass to buy groceries. We did not go into town often. I stayed home with the boys and had gotten up early to feed everything, as usual, and since it was Saturday was sitting there listening to the horses eat when a strange thought came to me. I thought, "Could you leave all of this?" I looked around at the barn, horses, cow dogs, round pen, house, five acres, cowboying, everything, and wondered if I could. I had never had such a thought, but I pon-dered it a while and then surprised myself with the answer, "Yes, I think I could."

My answer was more like a dare than anything else, and it bothered me. I went back in the house and laid down on the couch to think about things. Ben and Dan were still asleep, and Beth had already gone into town, so I was alone and troubled by what had just happened.

Before I go on, I need to explain something that was very common to me but may not be so common to some readers. I had learned that different parts of the country gather cattle in different ways. The way that I had learned was on the large ranches in South Texas. The way that cattle are gathered on most of these large ranches was called "combing and drifting" the cattle to the pens. Cowboys ride or they trailer their horses to the far end of a pasture. The cowboys spread out and start combing through the pasture, drifting the cattle that they come upon towards the pens at the other end of the pasture. Everyone is supposed to end up at the pens about the same time and the cattle are penned.

In most of these pastures the brush is thick and cowboys are spread out as they work toward the pens. So the cowboys on either side of you may be 100 yards or more away. It is important that everyone stay together as they move through the pasture so that cows do not circle around and get behind you as you are drifting them to the pens. The way cowboys stay somewhat together and moving in the same direction is by hollering back and forth from time to time. It is more of a high pitch than a low pitch sound and is short and I guess spelled out like this; "wooo."

Whenever a cowboy hears that sound he knows that the other cowboy is wondering where you are. Cowboys are never lost; it's just that sometimes they do not know where everybody else is. Calling out like that and having someone answer back gets everyone heading in the right direction.

There were times when I would jump a bunch of cows, follow them around in the brush, pushing them toward the pens, and then get turned around and not be sure if I was heading in the right direction. I would holler out like that and not hear anything. I would holler louder, get still, and listen and maybe way off hear a very faint answer, "wooo." I would fast-trot my horse in the direction that I thought the sound came from, answer back, "wooo," get very still, and hear the answer a little louder, and again, a little louder, and soon be back with everybody else.

There was no better feeling than to have been wondering if you were heading in the right direction and then to know for sure. Or let me put it this way; there is no worse feeling than to think you are heading toward the pens and to come out where you started out at the first of the day while everyone else is waiting for you at the pens! This hollering back and forth was second nature to me and something that was a weekly and sometimes daily part of my life; working cattle and calling out back and forth as we combed through a pasture.

Now back to August 7th. As I lay on my couch, thinking about that "Could you leave all of this?" question, suddenly I heard a faint "wooo," not audibly with my ear but spiritually in my heart. I was very still and kept listening and barely heard it again. I called back in the same way, "wooo," not with my voice, but in my heart, and listened again, and heard it again, but so faint I could hardly make it out.

I began to turn toward it, in my heart. As I turned I could hear it a little bit louder and clearer. I called back and kept turning and heard it louder and louder and clearer and clearer! Soon I felt as if I had turned 180 degrees, and the sound of it was as loud and clear as a bell. I knew what was happening to me, and I prayed. "Lord Jesus, I know what you are doing; You are calling me into the ministry, to become a preacher, to go a different direction with my life. And I will, Lord, I will. I will do whatever it is that You are calling me to do."

With my eyes closed, suddenly I saw on the screen of my mind the Lord surrounded by thousands of angels, praising Him and singing. I could not see any particular features or anything, but I knew that it was Jesus; there was no mistake about that. It was as if I was looking on from a distance. I did not know what to think about what had just happened, but I knew that God had called me into the ministry. I had accepted a new direction for life: God's direction for my life. I never thought about it much before now, but I guess by the spelling of that word you could say that God "wooed" me into the ministry.

When Beth got home I told her what had happened. She asked me what that was going to mean for us. I told her I did not know, but I did know that God had called me. She asked if this meant that we would have to move. I did not know. Maybe we could stay and keep working in the mission. I called my parents and told them.

That evening we had planned to go out to one of the ranches that I helped work cattle on for a bar-b-que and get-together with a few other families in the area. We went, but my heart was not in it. I was thinking of what had happened that morning. As the men sat around a fire sharing stories, I remember thinking, "I've already heard all of these stories. In fact, I have told some of these stories myself." Whenever a bunch of cowboys get together they share roping stories, bucking horse stories, wild cow-chasing stories. Not only had I already heard most of these stories, I had done just about all of what they shared in these stories. I remember thinking, "I've done all of this. This is not my world anymore."

The next morning, Sunday, August 8, I told Beth that I wanted to go to church in Eagle Pass. We called Brother Enriquez and told him that we would not be at the mission that morning, and we went to the

First Baptist Church in Eagle Pass. We had gone there often and the people knew us well. I had not shared with anyone other than Beth and my parents about what had happened to me, and that Sunday I was quiet and just listened.

The pastor got up to preach and said, "I am not going to preach what I had planned to preach this morning. Instead I would like to preach from Ezekiel 34 which tells us the difference between good pastors and bad pastors." I knew that the message was for me. That morning all I heard was the "… woe to you shepherds who only take care of yourselves … who muddy the water for the other sheep … who do not go after the strays nor take care of the sick and needy …" On and on he preached about how important it was to be a good shepherd and how serious it was to be a bad shepherd. It bothered me most of the afternoon.

Later that afternoon I told Beth that maybe we should go to church in Carrizo Springs that night. I was hoping that I would hear a message that was a little more encouraging. It was a little farther than Eagle Pass, but we had close friends there. As we got closer to Carrizo, I determined that I was going to share what happened with our pastor, Bill Stockton. We arrived only a few minutes before the evening service was to begin. Bill met us at the door and I said, "Bill, I need to talk to you, seriously." Bill said that it was not a good time since the service was about to begin, but that he would meet with me as soon as the evening service was over.

The service seemed to last so long. When it was finally over I went up to him and he said that he had forgotten that there was a deacons meeting, and if I could wait he would get out as soon as he could and we could visit. Our good friends, James and Nellie Breiden told us after the service that Beth and the boys could go over to their home since

James was a deacon and that James and I would come over there as soon as the deacons meeting and my meeting were over.

I sat out in my truck while the deacons meeting was going on in the church and went back and forth over what I should say and do. Several times I was ready just to forget the whole thing. I was about to start the truck and get out of there when Bill and James came out. Bill motioned me to come in, so I went in to his office. He said, "Bubba, James and I left the deacons meeting early because we could tell you had something serious on your mind. So, what is going on?"

I did not want to share what had happened, but I took a deep breath and started talking. I struggled through the experience not realizing how emotional it was for me to relive it and share it with others. As I shared I began to cry and noticed that tears were also running down both men's faces. When I finished sharing Bill said, "Bubba, you have been called by God into the ministry. You will need to go back to school. Becoming a pastor means that you will enter a lifetime of study." I had not done too well in school and that was not what I wanted to hear.

Over the next few weeks I shared this experience with some of the men that I worked with and with some other pastors. I remember meeting with Brother Enriquez outside the mission. We sat down in old metal folding chairs in the Johnson grass and I shared with him my experience from August 7th. He cried as I shared with him and then said, "Bubba, don't do like I did and wait and not go back to school. Go back to school." I even drove up to San Antonio on a Saturday and met with Buckner Fanning, who was my parent's pastor at Trinity Baptist Church in San Antonio. Every pastor I shared my experience with said the same thing, "Bubba, you have been called by God into the ministry. Now you must go back to school." Buckner even said that he would help me by scheduling interviews for me at Baylor, Hardin-Simmons, and Howard Payne University. I knew that these were Baptist schools and were a whole lot more expensive that state schools. I did not know how I could go back to school and certainly did not know how we could afford it.

During those few weeks after my experience with the Lord, Beth and I struggled with what all of this was going to mean. One day I would really be down, and I would tell her that I just did not know how I could do anything else but cowboy. She would encourage me and tell me that I had better do what God wanted me to do and not what I wanted to do. The next day, she would be out in her flowerbeds working, and I would see tears dripping off her face and onto the ground. She would look up and say, "I don't think I can leave the place we have always wanted." I would assure her that we were going to pray and do what God would lead us to do.

We made arrangements to go to Waco, Abilene, and Brownwood over a Wednesday through Saturday trip. Buckner had made the appointments for us with admissions representatives in all three schools. We dropped Ben and Dan off at my parents house in San Antonio and away we went to Waco. We arrived Tuesday evening in Waco and got a room at a hotel next to Baylor. It was a nice hotel and we thought it would be fun to go swimming in the hotel pool. It had been a long time since we had gone swimming in anything other than the river, creeks, or stock tanks. A cement-bottom pool sounded like a real treat.

When we walked out to the pool I noticed that no one was there except one man, who was out in the middle of the pool. I jumped in and when I came up he started talking to me. He said, "Where are you from?" I said, "A little town on the border that you have probably never heard of." He said, "Try me." So I said, "It is a little place called El Indio." He said, "I have been there. What brings you to Waco?" I hesitated for a moment surprised that he had been to El Indio and also somewhat shy to share my experience with a stranger but decided to tell him just as I had been telling the others, and I did. He listened and then said, "You don't have to go back to school. You should stay down there in El Indio working in the mission (I don't remember telling him we worked in a mission). If you want a degree I can give you the address of a place in Arkansas that you can get a degree by correspondence, but you don't need a degree. You should keep doing what you love to do; cowboying."

For a moment I thought I could do just that, stay down there on our place, keep cowboying, and work in the mission. I wondered what in the world I was doing way up there in Waco so far from home in the middle of a cement pool with some stranger talking to me like I was some kind of long lost brother of his. This man bothered me. I thanked him for the information and moved away from him as fast as I could.

The next day we went in for our interview, and everyone was very nice. They looked at my transcript and said that most of the hours would not transfer because of the low grades. I told them that I was not proud of my grades at all, but I had been called into the ministry and had a new motivation now.

They said that Baylor was not an easy school to attend and that I could probably enroll for the spring semester but they could not make any promises. We got all of the information about making application, thanked them and left. I remember thinking that maybe we should just go on back to El Indio. I did not know how we could sell everything, move to Waco, and go to school. How would I provide for my family? Would Beth go back to work? What about Ben and Dan? Who would take care of them if Beth worked and I was in school? As we were driving out of Waco we stopped at a little hamburger joint for a quick bite to eat. There was a "help wanted" sign in the window. As we ate Beth said, "I could get a job here." I tried my best to picture Beth working there, the boys at some day care in Waco and me in school at Baylor, but I just couldn't do it. There was something wrong with that picture. In fact, it just about caused me to start crying to even think of it. We left Waco discouraged and drove to Abilene.

When we got out at the Hardin-Simmons campus I noticed a historical marker, which read, "Hardin-Simmons University began when a group of Baptist pastors and ranchers got together to meet the need for Christian education in West Texas for their children and cowboy preachers …" I felt like this place was started for someone like me!

We went in and met David Smith in admissions. The first thing he asked us was if Beth had worked before. We said yes, and he told her to go with him. Beth had worked at the Kleberg County tax office when I worked on the King Ranch back before Ben was born. That experience had qualified her for what was about to happen.

Away they went as I sat there in his office wondering what in the world was going on. In a minute he came back and explained to me that at Hardin-Simmons they had what was called the family plan, which meant that family members of university employees got their tuition paid for by the university. At the time I did not realize how significant that was, but I soon would. He said that there was an opening for a secretary.

Within a few minutes Beth came back in and said that she had been hired as a secretary for the university. David got all excited. Beth and I did not know for sure what was happening. David looked at my transcript and said that not all of the hours would transfer but some would and that I was accepted and could register for the fall semester if I could get back for registration on Tuesday, the last day to register for the fall term.

It was Thursday morning. I told him that I worked for the USDA, had five acres, horses, dogs, sons, and a lot of cowboy stuff. He said, "Bubba, you are who this school was started for. Our mascot is a cowboy. We have a barn for our six white horses (used in parades to represent the university) and you can store your saddles and stuff in the tack room. If you can get back here on Tuesday, you can start right away, and your tuition is already paid."

He also said that Dr. H.K. Neely, the dean of the School of Theology, wanted to meet us. The word had already gotten around to him through Buckner. I remember walking down to the theology building thinking, "Everything is happening too fast. I need to slow down." I heard in my heart God say, "Go on, Bubba, there is more." It was as if the Holy Spirit was pushing us along. I could feel His excitement and joy.

When we went into the theology building the secretary gave us the name of a lady who had a rent house not far from the campus. She said, "I heard that you may need a place to live and this place just came open today." We went in and met Dr. Neely and shared with him our experiences, and he said that he would be looking forward to seeing us in a few days at school for the start of the fall semester. We left, met the lady with the rent house, put down a deposit, and headed back to San Antonio where we picked up Ben and Dan, rented a moving van and headed back down to El Indio. It was Friday.

As soon as we got home I called my supervisor and told him that I was resigning and would not be able to give much of a notice. I had plenty of annual leave and sick leave and wondered if it would be all right if I used it for my notice. I shared with him how it all happened, and he said that he was not surprised. We started loading up the truck.

Some friends from Eagle Pass happened to be out driving around and thought they would come see us. We shared with them what had happened, and they stayed and helped us load our furniture into the truck. This same couple had helped us move in to Eagle Pass from Kingsville years before. I thought about that as they were helping us.

Gene Allen, one of the ranchers that I worked with quite a bit, drove by and saw the truck and stopped to see what was going on. He and I stood out in the barn and I shared with him the experience I had with the Lord. He asked what my plans were for the five acres and trailer house. I told him I had not given it much thought but would put it up for sale. He said that he needed a place like that to stay in when he was there and offered to buy it from me. I had not sold property before and did not know how it worked. He paid me the equity that we had in it and took over the payments.

As he wrote out the check, I noticed that tears were dripping from his chin. I also noticed that he added $1700 more dollars to the amount that we had agreed to. He said, "Bubba, the world needs good preachers. I want to help you with some spending money for books and stuff you will need to be a pastor. So, go out there and give'em *heaven!*" He also said that he would take care of my horses and dogs and that I could come get them or that he would sell them for me, but that I was not to worry about them. He would take care of them for us until we decided what to do with them.

Sunday we drove to Carrizo Springs for church. Bill had asked me to share with the congregation the experience that I had with the Lord on that Saturday. After the service several people came forward making commitments to Christ, and the church licensed me to the gospel ministry. I did not know exactly what that meant, but Bill explained that it would help with something called a "ministerial grant." I later found out that the tuition was only part of the expenses of going to school and this "ministerial grant" came in handy.

Monday morning we finished putting the last items into the truck and horse trailer and were ready to go. I put the key in the place where I told Gene I would hide it for him and told Beth that before we left I had to go out to the barn one more time. As I walked out there, I started to cry. I fed the horses one last time and stood there a minute, listening to them eat, and then broke down and really cried. I held on to the main cedar post in that old barn that I had built and cried so hard it was shaking the whole barn.

It wasn't that big of a barn, but it was one that I had built. I had hammered out the old tin and had sawn the broken ends off of the old lumber and had built it myself. As I held on to the cedar post crying, I thought to myself, "I just can't do this. I just can't do anything else but cowboy. I do not want to leave. This is everything we ever wanted. I can't leave it all." I was hugging that old cedar post tightly.

Beth came out, crying, put her arm around me, and said, "Come on, Bubba, let's get out of here before we both change our minds. We know that God has called you. All four of our pastors said you needed to go back to school. We can't stay here anymore. Let's do what God is calling you to do. Come on, let's go now." She literally pried my arms loose from that old post, and we walked out of that barn together, both of us crying. I got in the moving van, and she got in our truck with the horse trailer, and we both cried all the way to Abilene.

When we arrived in Abilene seven hours later at the house we had rented, we were exhausted. I backed the moving van up in the small driveway, turned the truck off, and sat there a moment. Then it felt like every ounce of energy left my body. I was tired from moving, tired from crying, tired from driving, and from everything happening so fast; just plain old dog tired. I half prayed and half talked to myself and said, "What in the world are we doing way up here in *Canada*! I can't unload this stuff. I don't have any energy left. I need some help."

Literally, before I said the word "help," a huge black man walked up to the truck and said, "You look like you could use some help." He startled me. I was not used to seeing any black people, and he was huge! I said that I did need some help and for the next few hours we unloaded the van. One of the mysteries in life is that things unload faster than they load.

He did not say much at all as we worked, and he could work. He was as strong as an ox and almost as big. As I went into the van for the last chair, I thought to myself, "I need to pay this good man something." But when I got off the truck, he was gone; gone as in nowhere to be found, gone. I looked up and down the streets and did not see anyone. I still believe to this day that he was an angel sent by God to help us. One day I will see him again in heaven, and we will talk about our unloading experience together.

The next day I registered at Hardin-Simmons University as a freshman and the following day I went to my first class. I felt so out of place. There I was, twenty-nine years old with a bunch of eighteen and nineteen-year-olds. All I had was my old boots and blue jeans, and they both had horsehair still on them! Beth went to work the next week, Ben went to kindergarten, and Dan went to the day care center. It was hard doing all of that so suddenly. We all got up early and stayed up late, which was just the opposite of the way it was down in El Indio.

One morning as we were getting off to school, work, and day care, Dan, who was four at the time, said, "Daddy, where are the cow dogs and horses and our barn? I want to play in the barn. How long do we have to stay up here? Are we going to have to do this until Jesus comes back again?" I told him I hoped Jesus would come back today and that we would have to go roaming around on Saturday and see if we could find us an old barn somewhere. Taking him to the day care was the hardest part of the whole experience.

Those first few weeks were as hard as anything I had ever done. Shifting gears from physical cowboy work to mental school work was a real pain in the head. One day I remember having about an hour in between classes, and was so homesick for my old cowboy life I could hardly stand it. I thought if I could just go out and be around some horses and see my old stuff I would feel better. I drove out to the university barn where I had stored all of my cowboy stuff, but the tack room was all locked up. I started to get mad but then just broke down and started to cry again, like I had when we left El Indio. I remember thinking, "I sure have become a cry-baby since God called me into the ministry." Standing there with my head leaning up against an old wooden tack room door, crying, with my hat and boots and school books must have been quite a sight. During those first few months I guess I must have prayed, "God, help us" about a million times.

We quickly got into a routine. I got three different part-time jobs; cleaning the YWCA, picking up trash at the soft ball fields, and gathering information at the courthouse on drilling permits for an oil field rental company. I could take Ben and Dan with me on each of these jobs. When I was not in class, they were with me. They enjoyed it, and it made the work better for me. I was getting all kinds of inspiration in class but had no one to preach to, and so I would preach to Ben and Dan as we worked and to Beth when she would get home from working at Hardin-Simmons. I would follow her around preaching. She would occasionally turn around and rededicate her life, and I taught the boys to say "AMEN" at particular times while I preached.

Cleaning the YWCA building was the first of those jobs. It was across the street from our house. The head lady allowed me to work around my class schedule. I was to mop the downstairs, keep the furniture properly arranged, and clean the bathrooms whenever I had time during the day. I remember praying the whole time I would be mopping (in my hat and boots, of course), "Lord, please don't let any cowboys come in here and see me doing this."

After a couple of months of this routine, we began to get low on money. We were not making enough to keep up. Living in the city was more expensive than living in El Indio. One Saturday afternoon, Beth and I were sitting in the living room talking about what we should do. I told her that maybe I should drop a few classes and get another job. We decided to pray.

As we were praying, I heard the mailman put mail in our squeaky mailbox on the front porch. Getting mail at the house was something new to us because in El Indio and on most of the ranches where we had worked we had to drive to the post office to get our mail. Getting mail at the house was one of about three things we liked about living in town. As we prayed, asking God what He wanted us to do differently, I heard the mailman, and thought, "The mail is here; how nice." We said "AMEN" and got the mail.

There was a letter in the mail that day from the treasurer of the First Baptist Church in Eagle Pass with a check for $100. He said that a member had given it to him with the instructions to send it to me every month for as long as I was in school, which he did. We both cried and thanked God together, and I thought about that verse in Isaiah 65:24, that says, "Before they call I will answer; while they are still speaking I will hear." Six years later, the month after I graduated with a master's degree from Southwestern Baptist Theological Seminary in Fort Worth, the check stopped. I never did find out who sent that check all those years, but I have thanked God for them many, many times.

In January 1983, the Calvary Baptist Church in Rotan called me to be their pastor and we moved sixty miles north to Rotan. They provided us with a parsonage and an education in church work that supplemented my undergraduate work at the university. Beth stayed at home with the boys and we took out student loans and finished a B.A. degree in Bible with a minor in Spanish two and a half years later.

In December of 1984 the New Prospect Baptist Church in Nemo, a small community a few miles east of Glen Rose, called me to be their pastor and we moved to their parsonage, a small house on thirty acres, with a barn. I was able to complete a master's degree at Southwestern Baptist Theological Seminary while we lived and pastored in that community. Later God allowed me to complete a doctor of ministry degree in 1999 from the same seminary with a project in Uganda, East Africa among village pastors.

During the past twenty-five years (1982–2007), we have lived in six different places. I have been the pastor of six churches. God has allowed us to go on mission trips to five different nations of the world on three continents. He has shown us what revival and church growth are, allowing us to take part in ten new churches being planted and built. We have seen people saved, healed, delivered, revived, changed by the power of God to love and serve Jesus Christ, and countless miracles and answers to prayer. We have seen His face shining through the faces of blind orphans as well as multimillionaires. And it has only been twenty-five years since we left El Indio, with horsehair still on our clothes and boots.

I think about that little place we had in El Indio from time to time and the cowboy life that we lived there. We had moved from ranch to ranch and from job to job to finally get there and had worked hard to fix it up just like we liked it. I had horses, a few head of cattle, cow dogs, round pens, saddles, and a barn made from second hand tin and boards. Beth had her home, flowerbeds, and vegetable garden. Ben and Dan had their stick horses, haystacks, and dogs to play with.

Both boys are now married with families of their own. Ben is a general practice resident at Santa Rosa Hospital in San Antonio, and Dan is an orthopedic surgery resident at Scott & White Hospital in Temple. Beth went from planting and growing flowers and vegetables to planting and growing women's ministries and Bible studies in every church we pastored. She teaches God's Word and shares with ladies in retreats and conference settings. Her heart stays on the mission field, especially in Uganda. God has blessed us beyond words.

Sometimes I think about how tightly I was holding on to all of it, especially on that day when we were ready to leave it all there. I think about how I was holding on to that old cedar post in the barn and crying, not wanting to let go; holding on to old boards, tin, and cedar posts, and I tremble as I think of how close we came to staying there. The first year at school there were times when I thought we had really sacrificed for God by being there instead of back in El Indio. But now I see that if I had held on to that old post and not done what I knew God wanted us to do, we would have sacrificed everything for old boards and tin.

I don't know what the "cedar post" is in your life, but I do know this; God has abundant life waiting for those who are willing to make the exchange. There is no comparison between the things that God has prepared for you now, in this life, with those "old boards, tin, and cedar posts" that you have accumulated. Do whatever it is that God is calling you to do today. Trust Jesus Christ; live now the way you plan to live in heaven; be obedient to God no matter what it costs, and know this for sure; it is not what we do that counts, it is what *Jesus Christ has done* that will last! And He invites us to trust Him and to receive what He has done for us. When we do, He glorifies God and others are blessed. That is why I say, ***"To God be all the glory; great things He has done!"***

The Old River Rider

Working down on the Rio Grande allowed me to meet some interesting people. One of the men I worked with was named Tom (name changed to protect the guilty). Tom was about 60 years old when I knew him back in the late '70s and early '80s. He was raised several miles outside of Uvalde, Texas. Tom and his brother graduated from Texas A&I University in Kingsville, but many people did not know this because when you were around them you would think they never graduated from elementary school. Actually, Tom earned a master's degree in biology and taught school down in south Texas.

Tom went back to working on ranches after a few years of teaching so he could stay out in the country and live the simple, good life. Looking at Tom was like looking at an old photograph. He was about six feet and weighed about 200 pounds. He was built stout, with strong, wide shoulders, and was slightly bow-legged, which was especially noticeable when he was wearing his chaps. Tom always wore a wide-brimmed hat with a leather stampede strap, and most of the time he wore a red or blue bandana around his neck.

He hired on with the USDA in Eagle Pass, Texas, as a river rider. Tom had thirty miles of river he was responsible for patrolling on horseback. He bought twenty acres several miles outside of town, pulled an old trailer house out on his land, and lived the way he was raised. We would call the way he lived "roughing it," but he called it normal.

Tom would leave the windows and doors wide open most of the time with chickens, dogs, cats, and even a pig now and then wandering in and out at their leisure. He would eat without a shirt and preferred to sit outside under an old tree in his front yard. Of course, there was no grass around the house, but Tom did not mind at all. He had his barns and corrals, his horses and dogs, a few head of cattle, several goats, a milk cow, chickens, pigs, and even a few guineas.

Tom was a cowboy, horse trainer, horseshoer, hog hunter, fruit tree grafter, and expert in different types of bugs, birds, and edible plants and roots. He chewed tobacco all day and ate garlic pods to keep the mosquitoes and chiggers away. He also said that garlic was good for your heart. It was a chore to stay in the same truck with him. Those that did learned quickly how to breathe through their mouths. His trailer house was so open that you did not notice it much when eating with him, but it was hard to be cooped up in a closed space like a pickup cab with Tom.

Every chance he had, he would load up his horse and dogs and go hog hunting. His dogs were good at working cattle or hunting wild hogs, although sometimes they would get mixed up and gather a bunch of cattle right in the middle of a good hunt. Tom would go into Eagle Pass once a week to turn in his paper work and occasionally would go across the river into Mexico for some entertainment and recreation.

On one of his trips across the river into Piedras Negras he met Maria, his future wife. They fell in love and decided to get married. Tom named her "Big Mama" because she was both big and already had children when they met. She brought her children with her and moved in with Tom. They were one big happy family.

Occasionally I would help Tom patrol his territory, work cattle, or help him catch a wild Mexico horse or cow that had strayed across the river. It was an experience to eat lunch (sometimes supper) at Tom's with Big Mama and the whole crew: kids, chickens, goats, and a small pig or two. I never was sure just how many children they had because there were hers, theirs, and usually some of her relatives' kids around, and they were never still enough to count. We would eat stuff they had grown and raised sometimes as fresh as twenty minutes old. Big Mama was a good cook and put up with Tom's ways without any complaints.

This story was told to me by a friend, Bill, who also worked with us on the river. Tom had asked Bill to join him on one of his hog hunts one weekend. It was a cold and drizzly day, which is good hog hunting weather. Dogs are able to run farther and stay on the trail longer on cold, damp days. Bill loaded up his horse and went to Tom's place early on a Saturday morning. Tom's trailer was hitched up to his old pickup truck when Bill arrived. As Bill was putting their horses into Tom's trailer, Tom started beating on the side of his truck yelling at his dogs to load up. Four or five dogs jumped in the bed of the pickup, when all of a sudden here comes Big Mama with her kids and her sister along with two or three of her kids.

Bill looked at Tom in disbelief and said, "They are not going with us are they?" They were. Tom said they wanted to visit the family that worked on the ranch where they were going to hunt. Before Bill could object, Big Mama, her sister, and several children ages 8-11 were all climbing into the back of the truck. What a sight: Tom and Bill in the cab, horses in the trailer, wet dogs in the back of the truck, and Big Mama, her kids, her sister and her kids all huddled up next to the cab in the back of the truck, in the cold and drizzling rain.

After a few miles the heater in the cab of the pickup was good and hot. Tom had already eaten several pods of garlic and had a jaw full of chewing tobacco with a used spit cup on the dash. Bill was breathing through his mouth, but what was really bothering him was Big Mama and her sister with all the kids shivering up against the cab in the back of the truck. Finally Bill could stand it no longer. He said, "Tom you have got to pull over and let them get in here with us. They are shivering back there." Tom said, "Oh Bill, settle down. Them dogs are used to riding back there. I don't never let them ride up here with me! They smell bad!"

In 1982 God called me into the ministry, and we began to make plans to move to Abilene. Tom was with several other cowboys when I shared my experience with God. Tom knew that Beth and I were churchgoers because he knew we worked in the El Indio mission, but he and I had never talked about the Lord. As I shared the events of that day on August 7th, 1982, one of the cowboys got up and said, "That is the craziest thing I have ever heard. You are leaving all of this to go back to school and become a preacher!? You don't make any sense at all!" Tom interrupted him and said, "You shut up and sit down. Bubba is not through telling us something important. Whenever a man hears God speak, it is the only thing that makes sense! And I think Bubba is going to make a darn good preacher!" Tom used another adjective to describe the kind of preacher he thought I would be and never used the word "darn" as far as I know. Then he looked over at me, winked, and said, "Tell us what happened next."

Several years after we left El Indio I received word that Tom died of a heart attack. He was at home by himself when it happened. I believe I will see Tom again, and in heaven, out under a big tree, we will sit down together and will talk again. And he will wink and say, "And so, tell me what happened next."

The Spotted Bull

I enjoyed cowboy work, especially when we needed to rope something about half-wild. I never did like roping in an arena much but did like roping out in the pasture. There was something exciting about chasing an old mossy-back cow through the brush and then catching her out in a small opening.

There is just nothing like running through the brush after an old cow or bull on a good horse, with a medium size loop in one hand and the rest of the rope and reins in the other, ducking mesquite limbs, jumping cactus, whooping and hollering and hitting a cleared place just in time to settle your loop over the critter's head or horns. Then letting them hit the end of the rope and feeling the pull of that wild thing bouncing around on the end of your rope, with leather creaking and your horse snorting. There is just nothing like it, if you like it; and I liked it. I miss it.

Most of the time after roping the old cow or whatever you caught, you would work your way back to a road or trail and wait for the trailer to arrive. Then you could drag the cow, bull, or calf into the trailer, jump your horse into the back end of the trailer and either head to the pens or look for more loose cattle. Other times you would need to throw down whatever you had roped and tie him with hobbles or to a small tree by the horns with a neck rope. Then you could go get the trailer, drag him in, and head to town. I always carried some hobbles and a few tie ropes with me and was always ready for a good chase.

One of the ranchers down in El Indio, where we lived at the time, had a large brushy pasture leased close to the town site of El Indio; in fact, it bordered the last street of the town. There were only about nine square blocks or so in El Indio, and it would be a stretch to call them streets since none of them were paved. Anyway, this pasture was the only way to get from the highway down to the stretch of river I rode. I would guess this pasture to be about 400 acres. There was a decent road running through the middle of this pasture. It had a brushy creek also running down the middle of it with a medium size tank of water at the far end, close to the river. There had not been any cattle in this pasture for a long time because of the thick brush along the creek. Cattle would get down in there and were hard to get out.

One day I decided to roam around the pasture and see what I could see. I found the tank of water and started to ride up the creek. And about half way up the creek I found some cow tracks, two sets of tracks to be exact, one larger than the other. I first thought the tracks might have been Mexico cattle that had come across the river, so I went for some help. We jumped them out of the brush long enough to see that they were not Mexico cattle but belonged to the rancher who had the pasture leased. It was an old wild cow and her spotted bull calf. The rancher told us he had missed her when he had gathered the pasture two years earlier, and they were plenty wild, especially her spotted bull calf. He had never been in a pen or been anywhere near a man. The rancher said he had nothing but trouble out of this old cow and figured she was dead since he had not seen her for so long. The spotted bull was about two years old and was wilder than his old mama.

One day we decided to take some dogs with us to see if we could flush them out of the brush and catch them. We looked and chased, looked and chased, for most of the day without any luck. We would find them but they were smart and would head for the thickest brush and then stop. The dogs would go in after them, barking at them and bothering them while the old cow and her calf would just hold up in the brush. After a while the dogs would give up on us and come out panting and looking at us like they couldn't figure out why we were sitting there. Finally the old cow made a move and hit a clearing and one of the other cowboys got a rope on her, and we dragged her into the trailer, but not the spotted bull. He got away. He was wild, and now on his own, wilder than ever.

A few months went by, and I was heading out from the river through that pasture when all of sudden I came up on the spotted bull in the most cleared part of that pasture. He immediately started for the brushy creek as I was unloading my horse, Old Whiskey. Old Whiskey was my good horse. He was tall, stout, fast, and had a lot of cow sense, which means he could stay with cattle on the run by himself. We were able to cut this bull off from the creek, and I got a loop around one horn and his head. We called this catching half a head. Bulls would sometimes choke easy if roped around the head only, and could pull you all over the pasture if you roped only around their horns. Half a head was a perfect catch for a bull. Most cowboys already know this kind of stuff.

This spotted bull had horns that went straight out and was about 800 pounds, and he was wild. He bounced around on the end of that rope bellowing like a young calf, and then got mad. He chased us around for a while and I started wondering how I was going to tie up this bull. Whiskey was managing to stay clear of his horns and I was managing to keep the rope from getting all tangled. We worked him over to a medium size mesquite tree and snubbed him up close to the trunk. Whiskey and I had him just where we wanted him.

The next move was tricky. We circled the tree about four times and had old Spot snubbed up tight. While he fought the tree trunk, I got my rope loose from the saddle in order to run up and take a quick half hitch on the rope keeping the bull on one side of the tree with me on the other. Then I could take my time and get a good tie rope around his horns using the tree as a shield, tie him up to the trunk, go get help, and load him right up. That was how it had worked in the past, but this time something went wrong. The bull didn't cooperate.

When I ran to get the half hitch on the tree, he started coming around the other side of the tree, meanwhile coming unwound from being snubbed up close to the tree. This was not good because I had taken my rope loose from the saddle, and Whiskey had walked away from the action to graze a little. There I was on one end of the rope with the spotted bull on the other end and with only about three wraps around a mesquite tree, and him unwinding around the tree to get at me. I was running around the tree as fast as he was running around trying to get me. I guess you could say that his first experience with a human was not good, or another way to say it was, he was mad.

I could keep the tree between him and me with enough wrap to hold him, but my chaps slowed me down, and I started getting winded. It must have been a sight to see although Whiskey did not seem interested in the least. Every time the bull started getting close to me, I would back up and let him go under the rope but would lose a wrap. I knew that before long I would lose my advantage and not be able to hold him. I was trying to decide when to turn loose, lose my rope, and make a beeline up another tree.

Somewhere around the time I lost the second wrap, and trying to keep the tree between old Spot and me, I started praying. With only two wraps on the tree between me and old Spot and disaster, with some slack between his head and the tree, chasing me round and round, I was about to lose another wrap when suddenly, he stopped. With his sudden stop, my momentum carried me around to where I was almost face to face with him. He snorted and came at me from the other direction, which wound him up tighter to the trunk than before. This was what was supposed to happen the first time but he had gone the wrong way. I quickly got the half hitch on the rope up close to the tree trunk, and then sat back and watched him fight the tree, unable to unwind any more.

I sat there a while catching my breath, thinking how much harder it is to run with chaps on, and amazed at how it had almost not turned out so well, and I prayed again, mostly saying "Thank You God, for causing Old Spot to stop." I took my time in getting the tie rope on him, got my rope off his head, loaded up Whiskey, and went for some help. The rancher came with his trailer in a few hours, and we loaded him up without any trouble. After we started back I got to thinking about how close old Spot came to chasing me up that tree!

Sometimes worries, doubts, and fears can be like the spotted bull: always there, but elusive and hard to pin down. At other times you get all tangled up with them, going round and round, wondering what might happen next. And then you pray, and suddenly God seems to step in and stop the whole mess long enough for you to come at it from a different angle, from the angle of faith in His promises. Once you turn to God in prayer, the whole situation seems to change and start turning in the right direction. Before long these wild fears and worries are tied up, loaded up, and hauled off. Thank You, God!

The Sinner of the Family

On August 7, 1982, God called me into the ministry. We were living down in El Indio, a small town south of Eagle Pass on the Texas/Mexico border. I was working for the USDA, catching Mexican livestock that would cross the river. But on that Saturday in August everything changed for the Stahl family.

Within two weeks we had sold just about everything we had and moved to Abilene where I enrolled in college. Beth had gotten a job on campus, Ben had started kindergarten, and Dan was in day-care. It was quite a change. A few months later, a small church in Rotan, Texas, called me to be their pastor. This was only about an hour north of Abilene, so we moved again, this time into the parsonage, and I started pastoring Calvary Baptist Church in Rotan, Texas.

I had been raised in church, but had never been a pastor before. I soon discovered it was similar to ranching. You feed and count, care for the sick and wounded, count again, go after the strays, and count some more. The whole idea is to keep everyone accounted for and healthy which multiplies the herd, or in my new role, the church. I enjoyed getting out and meeting new people and inviting them to church. I would take Ben and Dan with me on these visits, and they heard me share the gospel of salvation many times and saw several come to faith in Jesus Christ.

About this time, Ben turned six and began asking a lot of questions about getting baptized. This is the way most parents know their child is close to accepting Jesus Christ as Savior. Beth and I shared with him on a number of occasions but were trying to delay as long as we could, so we would be sure Ben was serious about this all-important decision.

One Sunday, Dan and Beth stayed home from church because Dan was sick with a fever, and Ben decided he would also stay home and help. When church was over, Beth met me at the door and said, "You need to sit down with Ben right now; he wants to be saved." I went into the living room of the parsonage and found Ben sitting in a chair, with Dan lying on the couch across the room.

Dan did not feel good and had that "feverish" look, but Ben was all eyes and ears and very attentive. I asked Ben what he was thinking, and he said he wanted to be saved. I shared with him the same gospel story he had heard me share many times; how God loves us and sent His Son, Jesus Christ, who died on the cross to forgive us of our sins and to give to us eternal life, if we would simply accept His gift of salvation into our hearts by faith. Ben said he did believe, and wanted to be saved. I remember looking over at Beth as she stood at the edge of the kitchen, wringing an old dishtowel while Dan watched from the couch. Ben said he was ready to pray and be saved.

Ben prayed a simple prayer of faith asking Jesus into his heart. When he said "AMEN," I looked over at Beth, still wringing that old dish-towel but now with tears rolling down her cheeks. I was about to say something when all of a sudden, Ben stood up as if he wanted to make some kind of announcement. He said, "Now, in this family there are three Christians and one sinner." I winced and looked over at Dan whose expression suddenly changed from "fevered look" to "something is wrong here." Dan sat up and said, "Who is the sinner?"

I had some fast theological explaining to do and managed quite well although Beth was the one who calmed everyone down the most. A few years later, Dan had his own experience with the Lord, but I will never forget the look on his face when his big brother, in a very indirect way called him the sinner of the family.

When I remember that Sunday in the Stahl house, I am grateful for the Christian home I grew up in and my dad who shared his faith with me. I remember how my mother, Louise Stahl, would whistle hymns we had sung on Sunday throughout the week. I knew that when we went to visit our grandparents we would go to church with them and them with us when they came to visit. I have often wondered who it was, way back there in my family history that was the first one to accept Jesus Christ and start the Christian heritage in our family.

I have thanked God for the person who led that relative to Christ and for all of the parents in our family that later led their children to Jesus Christ. The most lasting things in life are given at home, good or bad. Home is supposed to be the closest thing to heaven on earth, but it can also be the closest thing to the other place. The presence of Jesus Christ in the hearts of the parents and the children is what makes home like heaven. No matter who the sinner is in your family, make sure you know who the Savior is in your family; His Name is Jesus Christ.

T-Ball

We moved to Rotan, Texas in January, 1983. I was attending Hardin-Simmons University in Abilene, which is about sixty miles from Rotan. We were living there because a small country church had called me to be their pastor. It was my first time to pastor a church.

Ben, our oldest son, had just turned six. He came home from school one day and said some of his friends had invited him to sign up for T-ball. I had never heard of T-ball, but Ben was interested, so we went down to the school to register him in T-ball. As we were filling in the forms they asked me if I would like to be a coach. I said I did not know anything about T-ball, but they said it was easy to learn. They told me it was baseball for youngsters that were just starting to learn the rules of the game.

They gave me a set of rules, a box of blue caps, and a bag with balls, bats, three old bases, and an old tractor disk with a radiator hose stuck on the top of it. I could identify everything in the bag except the disk/radiator hose piece. I had to watch another team practice before I learned what to do with this piece of T-ball equipment. The ball is placed on top of the hose at home plate. The batter hits the ball without it being pitched. We were called the blue team and had the freedom to name our own mascot. At the first practice we named ourselves the "Blue Jays," and we had a "J" put on all of the caps.

The rules for T-ball were easy. This is a game to encourage six and seven year olds to begin playing the game of baseball. It is a fun game. The ball is placed on the "T" and the batter hits it off the "T" and runs to first base. It is just like baseball but without the ball being pitched. The rest of the rules are just like baseball but with this difference; every inning, every player bats. After three outs, you stop keeping score. After all of the players bat you switch, whether you have made three outs or not. Simple rules; fun game; encourages small children to learn baseball and have fun.

After a few games I figured out the simple strategy of making sure all of my players showed up for the games. Each team had twelve players. If all of your players showed up you could very easily make nine or ten runs per inning. It is much easier to hit and run at that age than it is to throw and catch. If your opponent had one player missing you could win, even if you did not make all the outs. But I also learned making three outs was more important than making a lot of runs because after three outs no more runs count.

Our first practice I learned we had twin boys, six years old, and their next-door neighbor, all three of whom had been playing catch since they were three! This was seen by some as unfair, but I saw it as the providence of God. I put one of those twins on pitcher's mound, where most of the balls are hit, one at shortstop, and their neighbor at first base. As the rest of our team was learning the basics, these three were making sure we got three outs early in each inning.

We had a lot of fun. Ben played second base. Everyone was learning to play baseball. We won all of our games. We had one game left to win before being declared the undefeated T-Ball champions of the world. We had to play the Golden Eagles who were also undefeated. Since baseball is such a big deal in West Texas, this was shaping up to be a big game. Our last game, was their last game; the only two undefeated T-ball teams in the county were about to meet.

The Saturday game finally arrived. This was my first rodeo in terms of coaching organized sports, and I had a growing desire to win, win,

win. Now, one of the things we are careful not to emphasize too much in T-ball is competition; it's a fun game. But I wanted to win so badly, I told my boys if we could beat this team, I would treat them to a T-bone steak and give them a college scholarship. They rubbed their hands together and licked their lips. Thinking back on it now, I guess the offer of a college scholarship was a bit too competitive, but they were not really that interested in it as much as the T-bone steak.

It was a close game. Back and forth went the score. Both teams had all of their players present, and I could see why they were undefeated. They had some boys that had also lived in the same neighborhood with the twins, and one kid looked to me to be about nine years old. He could hit it out into the outfield. My right fielder had not caught a ball all year (six games). He would wear his glove on top of his head. Once the ball did roll out to him, and everyone was yelling at him to throw it in. He threw it to his mother in the concession stand. Back to the championship game. They were ahead, and then we were ahead. There was a large crowd at this game and a lot of cheering; it was close.

We got down to the bottom half of the last inning. We were ahead by two runs, we had two outs, but they had two men on base, and their nine year old came up to bat. I could not prove that he was nine, but he sure was big for his age. There was a lot of cheering, and tension. T-ball is a fun game.

I was pacing up and down like a good coach should, but my boys were not handling the pressure very well. The boy out in right field sat down, with the glove on his head, and was crying. The others had looks of worry and fear.

Suddenly I realized we had already made three outs. I replayed the outs in my mind, and for some reason I think I was the only one who realized this fact. There was so much cheering and noise that it does get confusing with everyone batting every inning but not keeping score after three outs.

I jumped up and yelled, "Time out!" I think this was the first time anyone had ever called a time out in T-ball in Rotan. The umpire yelled back, "Time out!" The coach from the Golden Eagles got his rulebook out and was frantically looking to see if this was allowed. I called all of my boys out to pitcher's mound for a team conference.

My boys were a wreck. Some were crying, others had the look of hopelessness and disappointment, and others, just plain old fear. They said, "Coach, we have lost the game. Their big guy is coming up to bat, and they have two runners and …" I said, "Boys, listen to me. We are two runs ahead, they have two runners on base, *but we have already made three outs!*" They said, "What?" "That's right, remember here and over here, and the fly ball that Stevie caught? We are two runs ahead and we have made three outs; no more score; the game is over, and we are the champions of the world in T-ball!"

My guys exploded with excitement and enthusiasm. They threw their gloves in the air and shouted, "WE HAVE WON!" The other coaches did not know what was going on. They were still looking for some rule about "time out." I called my boys back into a huddle and said, "Okay now, calm down. Remember the rule; we stop keeping score, but they still need to let everyone bat. But the score is in, and we have won! So, get out there and have some fun. *You are the 1983 World Champions of T-ball!*"

All of their worry and fear disappeared. They got down in their game positions and started chattering at the big kid, "Come on, big boy, hit it as hard as you can." It made the nine-year-old mad. He hit a high fly ball out to right field. We all watched as my right fielder, wearing his glove, suddenly slipped his glove on the wrong hand at the last minute and caught it underhanded to the roar of the Blue Jay's side of the stands! They threw the ball around the bases in celebration of the victory they knew they already had. Next batter. Grounder to shortstop. He scooped it up with a little in-field dirt for effect and threw a bullet to first base. "He's out." More cheering and celebration. Batter after batter, out, out, out, out. The Blue Jays were playing better and having more fun than they had had all season. After each out, around the horn, more celebrating, shouting "We are undefeated!" Finally, their last batter, a short fly to second base; out. We all ran out to the pitcher's mound for a quick chorus of "We are the champions of the world." Then over to the bar-b-que pit for T-bones and soda pop. I will never forget it.

I still have the team picture we took that day, and the game ball with their names written on it. I keep it in my office at church. When I see it, I am reminded of how a team was transformed when they believed the coach that day. When I told them we had already won, they were not afraid anymore. They played better than they ever had before and had more fun than ever before. They played from victory and with victory rather than trying to gain it. They believed they were champions because their coach told them they were.

We have already won in Jesus Christ! He lived life victoriously and then on the cross gave us His life. God raised His Son from the dead on the third day to settle the score forever. Accepting Him by faith and living His victorious life gives us confidence, assurance, and peace in the midst of any storm. In Christ, you have already won. You are victorious. Whatever you are facing today, know this; Jesus Christ has already faced it, defeated it, and offers you the victory over it, in Him. We still have to face the heavy hitters, but we are not afraid any more because in Christ they are all defeated, and we have won! When you live life from victory, it's fun.

"All I Could See Was a Tiny Head"

The first church that I pastored was Calvary Baptist Church in Rotan, Texas. Rotan is considered West Texas. You know that you live in West Texas if you can see evaporative coolers hanging outside of a window of the house and at least once a month your teeth grit with sand from a sand storm. You also know you live in West Texas if everyone greets you on the road by waving at you.

I will never forget the first time I saw the northern sky turn dark red. I asked one of the deacons what it was, and he said, "It's Lubbock, and it's heading our way." It was the first time I had seen it rain red mud. There is no place like West Texas.

Calvary Baptist Church was a mission of the First Baptist Church back in the 50's, during the days of revival and church growth in our nation. It was a small church on the edge of town. The first Sunday I was there we had about 35 in Sunday School and 40 in worship service. After the evening worship service they voted to call me as their pastor; 30 "yes" votes, and 0 "no" votes. I was in my first year at Hardin-Simmons University and had just moved from El Indio a couple of months earlier. Up until that point, all I had done was cowboy. I had a blue sport coat for church, and wore boots all the time. In fact, I did not even own a pair of shoes.

One of the things that we shared with the First Baptist Church was the Sunday afternoon nursing home service. There were two nursing homes in Rotan and every Sunday we would be in one or the other, leading the afternoon church services. We would gather in the meeting room and sing hymns for about twenty minutes. Most of the people would come in shuffling or in their wheelchairs during the first ten minutes, and we would continue singing another ten minutes or so. Afterwards I would preach for about twenty minutes, and then we would visit in the rooms. We would not get around to all of the rooms each time but would try to visit with as many as we could.

One of the Sundays that we were doing our nursing home service, I had an experience that I will never forget. We had finished the service and were going around visiting in the rooms. The sights and sounds and smells of most nursing homes are unforgettable. As we walked down the hall, I happened to look in one of the rooms and the sight stopped me and caused me to look again. I could see what looked like a small, grey head but no body.

I knocked at the open door but the person did not respond. I went in and looked and could see that there was a body under the sheets but it was so small and frail that the arms and legs only made wrinkles in the covers. The small gray head with unkept hair was facing the wall with eyes tightly closed.

I could tell by the few pictures that this was a lady, and I asked one of the nurses if she had family. The nurse said that she did not have any close family and that it had been a long time since anyone had visited her. The nurse said that the lady did not recognize anyone anymore and was hardly ever awake. I went to her bed and leaned over and called her by name and said that I was a preacher and was going to pray for her. She did not respond, so I very gently put my hand on her frail little head and began to softly pray, but with my eyes opened.

As I prayed I could see her lips begin to move. I stopped praying and leaned closer so I could hear what she was trying to say. She never opened her eyes and spoke in a faint whisper. She said, *"I was eight years old ... we were under the brush arbor ... my mother was playing the piano ... the preacher was preaching on the cross ... I went forward and ... "* and then her words faded even though her lips kept moving.

As I left her room that day I prayed for her, thanking God for her testimony and for those who shared Christ with her and taught her the Bible. I also prayed for myself, asking God to keep me and to grow me into the kind of person that would glorify Him automatically and consistently with my words and actions, without even thinking about it.

We are to live each day the way we intend to live and love in heaven. Our life now is a school, preparing us for heaven. When we learn to do what Jesus has commanded us to do, we are then able to teach others to do all that He has asked of us. As we consistently live that way, our words, thoughts, and actions will become automatic, and we can live that way without thinking about it much, similar to the way we learned to drive. I have heard that people who play the piano all their lives are able to play long after they recognize anyone or know what they are doing. They have played for so long, the music has become a part of who they are.

In the nursing home that day, I wondered how many times that lady had shared those words, *"I was eight years old ...,"* and how many times she had blessed others with her testimony as she did me that day. What about you? Do you have a testimony about when Jesus Christ came into your life? Can you share with others the difference he has made in your life? Your testimony is the most important thing in your life. It is the thing to hold on to even if you have to turn loose of everything else. The only way to hold on to the things of God is to share them with others. Be sure to share your testimony with someone today.

Bibles, Bedrolls, and a Can of Potted Meat

In 1983 our church, Calvary Baptist Church in Rotan, went on a mission trip with the Hispanic church in Rotan. They had made plans to go down to Santa Elena, a border town across from the Big Bend National Park in West Texas. Santa Elena had a small mission church and had arranged for the mission team to have vacation Bible school and evangelistic visitation during the day and revival services at night. Four of us from our church went along for the ride and to help out wherever we could. Our team consisted of a college student, another man my age (about 30), his thirteen year-old nephew, and me. I had only been on a few mission trips prior to this, and the others were rookies, but we were all eager and ready to serve.

We crossed the border in a small boat. I was a little hesitant about this because I had worked for the USDA along the border at Eagle Pass only months before and knew that this was considered an illegal exit from our country and an illegal entrance into Mexico since it was not through a port (across a bridge). But we were "along for the ride" so I did not object and felt safe since we were with our Hispanic friends from Rotan.

We arrived late in the day and did not have time to do much except to unload and set up at the mission church in Santa Elena. It was dark before we knew it, and the four of us did not have a home assigned to us so we unrolled our bedrolls under a shed beside the church. The next morning as we were eating breakfast, some from our group asked if we wanted to go with a man named Juan into the interior to visit some other mission churches for a few days. We agreed and within the hour were in a Chevy Blazer with Juan and his eight year-old son Felipe. The only things we packed were our Bibles, our bedrolls, a box of saltine crackers, and a can of potted meat. I asked Juan what we would eat, and he told me that the Christians we were going to visit and encourage would provide for us.

For the next ten days we traveled all over that part of Mexico, going from village to village, preaching and teaching, sleeping in the homes of Christians, in small adobe church buildings, and eating what our hosts would cook for us. Some days we would visit as many as five of these places and sometimes only two, spending long hours on cow trails and bumpy roads. We were never on any pavement or anywhere near electricity or running water. It was like going back in time and was quite an adventure.

One day was especially interesting. We had visited two villages preaching and encouraging the believers and had plans to end up in another village late in the evening to visit one Christian lady and, of course, have a place to eat and sleep for the night. When we arrived at her village we learned that this lady had been gone for several days. I noticed that Juan was disturbed by this news. He told us we would try to gather some people up for a street service in hopes of someone getting saved so we could have a place to stay for the night and some food to eat. The next village was several hours away, and it was not safe to travel at night.

We tried to invite some men to join us for a street service but were insulted, mocked, pushed around, and told to leave. We walked to the other side of the square, but some of the men followed us and stirred up the people there also, and we were ordered out of town. They said they did not want to hear the gospel and were not interested in receiving

Jesus Christ. Again we were pushed around, and Juan said that we had to leave.

We drove outside of town and stopped beside a small mesquite tree. I will never forget it, as we sat down under that tree in the dust and opened up the can of potted meat and some crackers and ate supper as the sun went down. I could tell that Juan was worried. I did not translate his prayer for the others because he was praying for our safety from harm for the next leg of our journey. He said we would not arrive at the next village until after midnight. "Let's pray that those believers will be home," he said, as we got ready to leave. As we were about to get into the blazer he said, "Knock the dust off your feet as you get in and let's pray that this town will be open and receptive to the gospel the next time we come through here." And we literally did just that.

It was a long and slow trip over rough country, and we did not talk much that night. About one o'clock in the morning Juan said we had arrived. By the moonlight, I could see a few adobe houses in between two small mountains. Juan was honking his horn as we came to a stop while people, dogs, and a few goats came running out to meet us. Juan was happy and the people acted like he was a long lost relative. We all said our hellos, and I was ready to find a place to lie down and go to sleep. But an old man came running out with an old guitar and Juan said that they wanted to have a service, right then.

I told Juan we were tired and we would have the service first thing in the morning, but they were already setting up a place in a small courtyard for the service. It was about 1:30 in the morning. Juan said these three families were all believers and they had not had a preacher come by there in a long time, and they were hungry for the gospel and teaching from the Bible. So we had a service.

The old man played his guitar, which had two strings missing, as we all sang some hymns and choruses; then I preached and by about 2:45

we concluded the service. One of the men, who looked like the leader of this clan, spoke at the end of the service and prayed. I could understand enough Spanish to be deeply moved as he thanked God for such a wonderful midnight surprise and for stories from the Bible that they had not heard before.

Before unrolling our bedrolls under the stars in the same little courtyard where we had just had the service, I got to talk with this man. He told me they lived on a large ranch and that he was the foreman. I told him about my ranch background, and he said he was planning to work the owner's cattle in the morning and wondered if I could help them. I was excited about the possibility of working cattle again, and asked him about the ranch. He told me he was simply the manager of the large herds of cattle and horses belonging to the owner. I went to sleep wondering about the owner and where he lived, and if I would get to meet him the next day.

At sunup, a few hours later, with roosters crowing, babies crying, and the smell of coffee and bacon, Juan said we really needed to stay on our schedule because the main group would worry about us if we got behind a day or two, and we could not stay to help work the cattle. I shared this with my Christian friend and he smiled and said not to worry; he did not have to work the cattle today. He said, "The owner gives me much freedom about working the cattle and is not worried about when things get done as much as how they are done."

We said goodbye and drove away waving, with dogs and children chasing us as far as they could. As we went around the side of one of those mountains Juan said, "You just met one of the largest land owners in this part of Mexico who has been a Christian for less than a year." I said, "But he told me he was the ranch foreman." Juan said, "When he received Jesus Christ he gave his heart and everything he had to God and now considers himself the manager of the ranch; God is the owner!"

When I think about those three families deep in the interior of Mexico, in between those two mountains, our midnight services with the four-stringed guitar, and our gracious host, I thank God for the way He loves us, changes us, and teaches us His ways. I think about how quick we are to give our hearts to Christ but then keep everything else in our control rather than trusting His. But if we will give it all to Him, we find we have not lost it but actually gained it, and that we never really had any of it in the first place.

Jesus Christ has not come to take life but to give us life. The only thing He takes away from our lives is the sin and destruction, and in its place gives us His life of love, joy, and peace that go beyond description. He gives us His Spirit to guide us in what we should do and to teach how we should do it. God does more than help us; He changes us. I saw the change He made in the faces of three families one moonlit night, down in Mexico in a village between two small mountains.

The Old Woman in Kenya

I met Derrell Monday soon after becoming the pastor of Calvary Baptist Church in Rotan, Texas. He was the pastor of the First Baptist Church in Rotan. I was a young pastor just starting out and did not know "sic'em from comeback" about being a pastor. He helped me with things like what to say and not to say at funerals and weddings, what to do when you ran out of things to say: practical stuff that pastors need to know. He also encouraged me to go on mission trips.

In 1997, at Derrell's invitation, my son Ben and I went to Kenya on a mission trip. Derrell was the coordinator of ten teams that were assigned different churches on the east coast of southern Kenya. Ben and I were assigned a church way out in the bush. It took several hours down dirt roads to arrive at the village where we would be staying for the week. The van dropped us off on the side of the road where a few of the church members were waiting for us. They carried our luggage and we walked another hour or so to the little village where the church was located. It was a primitive area with mud huts and thatched roofs. We pitched our tent right beside the pastor's little mud hut.

Actually, there were four mud huts in a circle around a common campfire. Of course, they did not call it a campfire; it was just called "the fire." The area was about the size of the infield of a little league baseball diamond. The pastor, his wife, and four small children lived in one of the huts. Another hut was the kitchen where the ladies prepared the meals. The third hut was for the older children, the three teenagers, and the last hut was for storing firewood and supplies. The fire area had a fire burning all the time. The ladies would take coals from the fire into the kitchen hut for cooking. The thatched roof of the kitchen hut was blackened with the constant presence of smoke. None of these huts had any covering over the windows or doors.

The huts were made with sticks about as big around as an average person's wrist set in the ground like fence posts in either a rectangle or a circle. I estimated the size of most of the huts to be about ten feet by eight feet, and the circle huts to be about eight or ten feet in diameter. In between these main-pole sticks were smaller sticks, about the size of broom handles, woven in and around the bigger ones.

The roof structure was much the same with a large center pole in the middle. I would call it the stack pole because it was larger than all of the rest. All of these sticks were tied together with strips of palm leaves. Mud was caked in between the cracks for the walls, and clumps of grass were tied together for the roof covering. The floor was the ground. In the middle of this hut compound, right next to the fire, was our tent.

The fire was the gathering point, like a living room. There were people around the fire talking and singing all the time. When I say, all the time, I mean all the time. We would go to bed each night listening to them talk and softly sing. We would wake up each morning to babies crying, roosters crowing, and people talking and singing around the fire. The women were constantly carrying water from the wells, wood for the fire, or coals from the fire into the kitchen. The men were always sitting around the fire talking. But we noticed that they also gathered wood or hauled water, especially after one of the women said something to them, which they did not translate for us. They also brought food in every day.

Our food consisted of a tasty root, beans that reminded me of cowpeas, melons, which happened to be in season, fresh coconut milk/meat, and a type of corn bread they called ugali (pronounced ou-gah-lee, with an accent on the middle syllable). Ugali was white and had the consistency of dried out grits. You could mold it in your hands, which is how they would eat with it. They used the ugali to scoop up the other food. It was the main course as well as the utensils.

We would also have chopped up chicken, but I learned later this was something they were doing just for us. Eating was a social event for them. Ben and I noticed how they enjoyed it. Their hands were as much a part of the process as their noses and mouths. We would call it playing with their food, but it seemed important for them to feel and shape the food they were eating, and they talked constantly while they ate. Ben laughed and said he remembered getting in trouble at the supper table for all the things they were doing: playing with their food, talking with their mouths full, eating with their fingers, and sharing the food off of their plates with others.

They would serve us first; then the men would eat, then the women, then the older children, and then the young children. This seemed strange to us. They explained to us that the men would eat first because they were the ones who needed strength to go out and get more food, then the women, because they were the ones who prepared the food. We noticed everyone would leave some food on their plates to make sure the next group had something to eat. The children had the leftovers, and every crumb was eaten.

We were only a few miles from the Indian Ocean. The climate reminded me of South Texas, humid, with similar sights and smells. I had worked cattle on the King Ranch and the smells reminded me of the cow camps near the coast, with food cooking on an open fire, the smell of grass, animals, palm trees, and the feel of sandy soil. I loved it, even though it was hot and very humid.

The eight days we were there were filled with visiting families in the surrounding villages, sharing our faith in Christ, and having services each evening at our tent around the fire. Our visitation group consisted of Ben and me, Justin, the pastor, who was our translator, about five church members (who insisted on carrying our backpacks and Bibles), and a group of six or eight children. We would enter a small village and ask for permission to speak. A group of people would gather around us, either under a tree or inside a hut, and we would share the story of Christ and God's love for the people. People would pray to invite Christ into their lives and then would go with us to the next village. By the end of the day we would have forty or fifty people in a parade back to our camp for the evening service, which would gather another hundred or so. I could write a whole book just on the experiences of that first trip to Africa!

We found people that had never heard about Jesus. They knew about the creator God, but told me they did not know much about Him because He did not bother them like the other gods. The sacrifices they made to the gods were in order to keep the gods away, so they (the gods) would leave them alone. But the creator God was both good and far away. They also knew what it meant to sin and knew it was not right, but did not know that sin was breaking the laws of the creator God. Their definition of sin was the things a person does that are wrong even though he knows to do better.

I will never forget the look on their faces as we shared with them how the creator God sent His only begotten Son, Jesus, to earth in order to save us from our sins and be with us to teach us not to sin. They leaned forward as we shared how Jesus lived a perfect life, helping others, teaching others the ways of God, and healing people. They frowned as we shared how the religious leaders and the political powers had Jesus beaten and flogged and crucified. Then their faces shone with delight when they heard how God raised His Son from the dead on the third day in order to share His life with us.

We told them how Jesus died and took all of our sins with Him into the grave and then came out of the grave alive and without any of our sins on Him. Their eyes were fixed on us as we explained how Jesus had buried our sins in His death, forgiven us, and offered us His life and relationship with God. They were eager to pray and receive Jesus Christ into their hearts, their lives, their families, and homes. But not everyone did. Some would walk away when it came to time to pray.

Once as we were about to pray, one of the ladies started to walk away, and one of the men started scolding her. Justin translated for us and said the man was asking her what was wrong; how could she walk away from such an offer? She said she had to discuss this situation with her husband and he was away. The man, who was now the preacher, asked, "If there was a rhinoceros running down the path towards you, would you need to discuss this situation with your husband?" Everyone laughed, as she did, but still she walked away.

In one of the huts we visited, a group of about ten gathered around us. I noticed an old woman in the corner of the hut. She caught my eye because we had not seen very many old people. She was lying on a mat on the ground with another lady sitting beside her. As we sat down, she asked for help sitting up and listened as we shared our faith with the group.

After we had finished, I asked if anyone would like to pray to receive God's gift of salvation. Everyone looked over at the old woman as if to get approval. She began to speak and the pastor interpreted for us. She said that when she was a young lady two other white men had come to her village, sat in her hut, and shared the same story. This was the second time in her life she had heard the story about God's Son, Jesus Christ, and his sacrificial death on the cross.

She talked about how interesting it was to her that now as an old woman she was hearing the same story. She had only seen white men twice in her life, once as a young lady, and now as an old lady. Both times they shared the same story! She said as a young lady she had not prayed to receive the gift of salvation from God, but after the white men left her village, during the night, she reconsidered their story. As she slept she had a dream, and in her dream her dead father came to her with a warning not to believe the story of the white men and to have nothing to do with them.

She would not pray with us but said she was so curious about having white men in her hut again with the same story and offer of salvation. I thanked her for allowing us to share and encouraged her to reconsider God's offer of salvation in Christ. We prayed for her and her family and traveled back to our tent for the evening services.

The next day runners from her village told us that the old woman had died during the night and her funeral would be the next day. We went to the funeral as many of the people from the surrounding villages did. It was an all-day event with everything you would think of in the cultural setting of the East Africa bush country. There were several groups of people who were dancing and singing tribal songs. There were "professional mourners" that wailed and cried the whole time. One group of men built the coffin, while another dug the grave, a huge hole big enough for the coffin and other articles belonging to the woman. And then finally, her body, placed in the coffin, was lowered into the grave and covered with dirt. I was deeply moved as the funeral grew in emotion to lowering the body into the grave. There was more grieving, wailing, fainting, shouts of anger, and crying than I had ever heard or seen displayed at a funeral or for anything. I remembered thinking this must be what Hades sounds like; weeping, wailing, and gnashing of teeth.

After we returned to our tents, during the night, I began to wonder about the old woman. I wondered if after we left, she might have reconsidered the offer of God. I began to wonder if maybe her curiosity about our visit was stronger than the influence of her dead father and if she may have reached out with child-like faith and received Jesus Christ as her Savior. As I lay in my tent, listening to the people talking and softly singing way into the night, I began to wonder if one day, in heaven, I would see that woman again.

I know this, I went to sleep that night amazed at how much God loves us, and how much He desires us to know Him and love Him. He sent missionaries with the gospel of Jesus Christ to a woman in Kenya, twice, once when she was young and again on the last day of her life so she could hear, believe, and have everlasting life. And I believe we will see her in heaven. She will be the one up close to the Throne, singing the loudest, "Amazing grace, how sweet the sound …"

Begging to Give

Beth and I went to Uganda the first time in August of 1998. We both fell in love with the people and the place and especially with all we saw God doing among the people. Uganda has been experiencing revival for many years because of the presence of the Holy Spirit and the faithfulness of God's people. The relationships we made on our first trip allowed us to go on several return trips.

The summer after our first trip, I went back to Uganda with our son Dan, and a good friend, Kemper Crabb. The pastors we met the summer before asked if we could come back and conduct pastor-training conferences in eastern Uganda. A team of five leading pastors from the eastern part of Uganda made arrangements for three pastors' conferences over a ten-day period. Our church got involved by raising money for food, travel, and a Bible for each pastor. The cost for one pastor for the conference was estimated at $15. We planned for about 400 pastors to attend. At the end of the ten days we had conducted five conferences with over 2,000 pastors and church leaders in attendance. We shared our food.

So many of the pastors in Uganda do not even have a Bible or if they do it is only a page or small piece they have found. I remember one old pastor had a Bible he had found which he had been using for many years. The first page was 2 Samuel 4 and the last page was Luke 10. I will never forget the look on his face when we gave him his new Bible; I told him he was going to love Luke 15, the gospel of John, Acts, the letters of Paul, Peter, James, and John. This story is about the first confer-ence we held.

Our first pastors' conference was held in Iganga, one of the largest cities in Uganda. Arrangements and permits were secured from city officials and a conference center was rented. They called it a conference center but we would call it a metal building in need of major repairs. It was about the size of a gym. On one end was a stage area and the other end had one restroom. The pastors ate, slept, and attended our sessions in the conference center. About 700 pastors and church leaders came from all around the area. Pastors from several denominations attended, as did many people from the city, including beggars.

One of the things we try to prepare people for when they go with us on these mission trips are the beggars. Beggars are common in Uganda, especially children, the elderly, and the handicapped, some of whom are sent out by their families to beg. Some are refugees from other countries, but others are orphans with no other means of buying food for the day, or the elderly, whose adult children have died from AIDS. In a nation where adult children are the only means of support for aging parents, and with AIDS almost wiping out the adult population, it is the elderly and the children who are left on the streets to beg. All they need is food for that day, about twenty-five cents worth.

But once you give to one, you suddenly become very popular. It is a difficult thing to see. The beggars all approach you with what is known as the "beggar look." They are slightly bent over, with both hands cupped together and extended out. They glance upward at you and make a mournful sound. Some are severely handicapped. Many are lep-ers.

After each session we would take a short break. During the break we would pray with people. We soon discovered that several church leaders were attending and were also asking for Bibles. Many were willing to buy them from us, even begging to buy them, but we only had enough for the pastors. It was hard to tell them we could not give them or even sell them a Bible because we had other conferences, and we needed to make sure we would have enough Bibles for the pastors. We learned that many people who were asking for a Bible could not read, but wanted one because they recognized it as a holy book and wanted one for their home, like a relic or idol. We also learned that others would take them and sell them on the street. We had to depend on the pastors who planned the conferences to know who was a pastor and who was not.

At the end of the final session we were saying good-bye to many of our new friends and praying for people, when out of the corner of my eye I saw her coming, with the beggar look. She was an elderly lady bent over and limping with the hard life she had endured. I was preparing to pray for her and to give her a small piece of money when I realized that she was holding a wadded up piece of money, extending it out like a beggar.

As she began talking I thought she wanted to buy a Bible. I did not know what she was saying but I could tell that she was passionate about it telling my interpreter of the great need she had, and I could see that she had a bill worth about twenty-five cents. I was preparing my speech about how we could not sell the Bibles, when my interpreter surprised me with her request.

As my interpreter started translating what she was asking, my eyes filled with tears. She passionately reminded him and me that we had forgotten to take up an offering, and she felt robbed of the opportunity to help offset some of the expenses of the conference. She was grateful we had come from America to share with her pastor and the others so they could have Bibles and training to lead the churches with, and she wanted to contribute to the cost of the conference. *She was begging to give!*

When she put the old wadded up, torn bill in my hands I felt like I had received a $10,000 bill, if there is such a thing. I realized this was money for food for one day. I understood some were willing to buy a Bible rather than eat that day, but her request simply blew me away. In an instant I was taken back to Luke 21 in Jerusalem and the last week of Jesus' life on earth. With all of the questioning and intensity of the moment, Jesus pointed out an old widow who put in two mites, which was all she had. Jesus said she had given more than all of the others.

As I held the wadded up bill, dirty and worn with age, I knew that God was going to multiply it and use it, and others would be blessed with it. We had certainly been blessed by her obedience and eagerness to give. I realized that God had blessed her with joy and an eagerness to give; her obedience had blessed us. Reflecting back on that moment and remembering the old woman and her humped back and bad hip, her wadded up money, and the joy in her eyes as she begged to give, has taught me important lessons on giving: it is not how much we give that counts, it is **how** we give that counts, and when we give with joy and eagerness, our obedience blesses others, and God is glorified.

Christmas in July

We lived in Boerne for twelve years, from 1992 until 2004. I was the pastor of the First Baptist Church in Boerne and saw the community and the church grow during those years. I think I grew more than the church and the community combined. It was a wonderful experience in every way.

One of the best things about our time there was to see the development of unity among the pastors of the various churches. We met every month for prayer and for fellowship and grew to respect and love one another. I believe God used these relationships to bless the whole community of Boerne. We had a common vision to see the families of Boerne blessed and become more and more aware of God's presence, His power, and His love for all people. We wanted to see Boerne grow spiritually the way it was growing numerically and commercially.

We were very much aware that the founding fathers of Boerne were not "church-goers." In fact, Boerne was begun by "free-thinkers" from Germany. The town was named after one of these "free-thinkers" even though he never went to Boerne himself. A "free-thinker" is someone who claims they are not restricted in their thinking by Christian beliefs and the Bible. Some would call themselves atheists.

In the early years of the town there was a sign at the city limits of Boerne that said, "Preacher, don't let the sun go down on you within these city limits." The first churches had to be built outside the city limits of town. Over the years the Christian influence of love had prevailed and the town had changed for the better, as towns should. The presence of God's people in a town is what transforms that town for the better, especially when God's people love and respect one another. The Church is the only hope for a community and becomes the source of blessing for that community.

It was during those years in Boerne that we started going on so many of our mission trips. The First Baptist Church of Boerne was, and still is, very missionary. This story is about one of those trips that we took to Uganda, East Africa. And all that I just said about the history of Boerne and the importance of churches in a community is important information for the story.

We had been going to Uganda for a number of years and had developed many wonderful relationships with church leaders and the people of that beautiful nation. The nation of Uganda has been experiencing revival for a number of years and has seen thousands of people led to faith in Jesus Christ and hundreds of churches started. Each year we would go and work with a church that would start a new church. We would provide training for pastors and church leaders and would go with them to an area where a new church was needed and help them "plant a church."

It was a wonderful experience for us to work all week along side of these beautiful Christians in leading people to Christ and then be with them on a Sunday morning to "open up a new church" with the new believers and a new pastor who had been attending the training all week. We would take money to buy property and materials for the new building (about $2500) and begin a relationship with this new congregation. Over the years we were able to see these new churches become "grandparents" as the revival continued and many new churches were started.

On this particular trip, we were working with a church that wanted to start a church in a community called "Nawango." Nawango was about a two-hour walk from the church we were working with. One young Christian man who lived in Nawango walked that distance every Sunday to go to church. He asked the pastor if the church would help him to start a new church in Nawango. There was not a church of any kind in that community of about 3,000 people. Nawango means "leopards" because there used to be many leopards in that area. There were many problems and needs in Nawango. The people told us that the people of Nawango were sad people, many of them suffering from what we would call depression.

And so on a Saturday, we traveled to Nawango to visit and share our faith in Jesus Christ in that area. Several of the pastors and church leaders had been in that area all week setting up a base camp for our group to spend the day and have our services. Our plan was to visit in the homes of the people, have a big evangelistic service on Saturday evening, and then another service Sunday morning and start a new church in Nawango with the new believers. Everyone was so excited, especially the young man who had requested his church to start the new church.

The pastors built a makeshift platform and cleared an area where several hundred people could stand and sit and hear the gospel. Tall trees surrounded this large, open area. We had purchased a small generator and one of the pastors had a keyboard someone had brought over from the States. They rigged up the keyboard and a sound system, found the electronic drums on the keyboard and several songs that had been programmed in the system and then turned it up real loud. It was funny to us from Boerne because the songs that were programmed in the system were not really what you would call religious songs, but they were played all day long, real loud, with drums. This of course was a draw for the people to come to the services and it worked very well.

All day, as we were visiting, we could hear the music of Elton John, the Beatles, the Beach Boys, the theme song to the movie *Titanic*, and other songs that we all liked but seemed strange to us in that setting. As we would be witnessing to some family, a new song could be heard and we (from Boerne) would laugh because it seemed funny to us to hear those songs as we were witnessing in this remote area of Uganda. We found out later that the people were amazed at how joyful we were and became interested in what we "had." We would invite them to the services and simply told them to go toward the music and we would have a great time together. Throughout the day we prayed with many, many people and all met back at the base camp for an early supper on Saturday evening.

People came from everywhere for the service. In fact, they came early for the supper. We had plenty of food and enjoyed seeing our new friends that we had met during the day with us for a meal. The keyboard and drums were going strong while hundreds of people gathered in our cleared out area. We sang, heard testimonies, and I preached from Haggai 2:7 on "the Desired of the Nations will come," a simple evangelistic message of the need that every person, family, and community has and the promise of God to send His Son, Jesus Christ to meet that need.

When it came time for the invitation I would always turn to my good friend and pastor, Wilson Gowa for the invitation. Wilson has been the pastor of Kakombo Baptist Church in Uganda for over thirty-five years. He was a young pastor when Idi Ammin was at the height of his reign of terror in Uganda, and Wilson was one of those who was tortured because of his faith in Jesus Christ and as a pastor. I love Wilson Gowa and I love to see and hear him preach, even though I do not understand the language, I do understand his spirit of love and Christlikeness.

Wilson gave the invitation. It is always an exciting and sometimes tense time when the invitation is given. Someone has to be first. Once that person steps out and makes a stand for Christ, the floodgates usually come open with many, many others following also making the same commitment. One old man and his wife were the first ones to come forward, indicating a desire for the "Desired of the Nations." Then another came, then another, and then whole families started coming.

The keyboard guy thought it would facilitate things if music was playing and so he hit the keyboard button for "songs programmed" and to our surprise *Silent Night* started playing. Over two hundred people came forward while *Silent Night* was being played. At first I laughed because I thought that *Just As I am* or some other hymn like that would be more appropriate, but then I thought, no, *Silent Night* is perfect following a message on the promise of God to send His Son and how Jesus was being born into the hearts of the people coming forward!

All of the pastors and church leaders counseled the new believers and then the celebration started. More food was served, the keyboard got louder, and the people started dancing. We had to leave to get back to our hotel (about three hours away) but later we discovered that even more people came for the "dance" and several more were witnessed to and saved. And they danced all night!

We got up early the next morning and traveled back for another service and to officially open up the new church. By the time we got there another crowd had gathered. We moved over under a couple of the large trees because the cleared out area had become pulverized into fine dust by the all-night dancing. You could tell the ones who had danced all night because they were still covered with dust.

We sang and spoke about how the community was going to be blessed by the new church. We ordained the new pastor and heard the first sermon. More people came forward to be saved. It was one of the most peaceful and blessed experiences I have ever had. As we sang and shared I remember small leaves from the trees gently falling around us and it was as if a powerful and peaceful Spirit was descending over us like a blanket. The people started sharing testimonies of how they now had peace for the very first time. The old man who came forward first stood up to share. I wept as our interpreter spoke to us the words that the man was saying.

He said, "Yesterday morning, I woke up as I had every day of my life, without hope, without joy, without peace, but I did not know why. Then some people from America came to my village and shared with my family about Jesus Christ. I asked Jesus into my heart and for the first time in my life I experienced peace and joy, and I danced all night! This morning the joy is still here in my heart and I now know why. What I have needed in my life all this time has come to me, Jesus Christ, the "Desired of the Nations" has now come to me, to my family, and to my village. Nawango now has a church. Peace has come to our village." Tears were running down his cheeks and ours as he shared. There was new meaning for me in the words of *Silent Night*, "sleep in heavenly peace."

The new members wanted to name their new church Nawango Boerne Baptist Church. They asked me what the word "Boerne" meant. I did not have the heart to tell them that it was a beer-drinking atheist from Germany, so I told them that it meant "little hills" since Boerne is in the hill country of Texas. I figured that I was not telling them a lie because when a person says "Boerne" people think of the hill country. They liked the name of their new church since there was also some "little hills" in their area as well; "Leopards Little Hills Baptist Church," has a nice sound to it. The past few years this church has started ten new churches in other villages in that part of Uganda.

Whenever I sing *Silent Night* at Christmas time, I think about that hot July day on the equator in Uganda and how the old man and the others came forward and a new church was born in that community. I think about how different a community is, no matter where it is in the world, because of the presence of Jesus Christ in His people. That community, no matter what the problems are that are in it, has hope, because of the joy that radiates from the people of God and because of the "Light" that shines from their hearts, driving back the darkness and changing that community for the better. I remember how the people danced all night with joy and I remember how the words "all is calm, all is bright, Christ the Savior is born," a Christmas carol from Germany, was sung by people from Boerne, while the people of Nawango were coming forward and being saved.

Wiasawa, the Twin

During the summer of 1998, Beth and I had the opportunity to go on a mission trip with several other mission teams from around the country to Uganda, East Africa. I was interested because I remembered that Uganda had suffered under the reign of terror by the dictator Iddi Ammin. He brutally murdered hundreds of thousands of Ugandans, most of them Christians, with thousands more tortured and maimed under his horrendous rule. I knew that many of those who had suffered this persecution were still serving in the church and I had never been around Christians like that, but I wanted to. I had also heard that Uganda, like other East Africa nations, was experiencing revival, and I wanted to see what that was like.

It was all that I had wondered but much more. Beth and I spent twelve days in a tent pitched beside a village church called Namatoke (which means "bananas") Baptist Church. We fell in love with the people and the country. I stayed an extra week after Beth and the others left to do follow-up work with the leadership from several of the stronger churches in that part of Uganda. We traveled to several of the churches and were able to give instruction to the new believers and encouragement and training to the church leaders.

The village churches in Uganda do not see as many "missionaries" as the city churches because the conditions in the villages are "primitive." There is no running water or electricity and the living conditions are rough. But the people are receptive to the gospel and new churches are springing up everywhere. For six years (1998–2004) the First Baptist

Church in Boerne sent us back each year to preach, to encourage the leaders, teach the new pastors, build new churches, start medical clinics with medical students that we helped through school that came out of these new churches; it has been very rewarding to be a part of. We have simply helped them to do what God has called them to do in their own country. We even helped them to build a seminary and trade school for the village pastors and church leaders.

On a typical trip we will set up our "camp" in the village and teach pastors and church leaders in the mornings (with Vacation Bible School for the children), then travel to a neighboring village that does not have a church in it for evangelistic visitation in the afternoons and then have a worship service in that village in the evenings, usually under a tree in the middle of the village. Village pastors and church leaders will come from all around the area and "camp out" with us for the week and, of course, help the host church in starting a new church in the near-by village.

It is a wonderful time of preaching, teaching, fellowship, and fun. The Uganda people are the happiest people in the world and the most joyful. Then on Sunday morning, at the end of the week, we start a new church with the new believers from the visitation and nightly services, with a pastor who has already been trained and committed to lead the new congregation. Being present for the first worship service of a new church deep in the "bush" with people that you have seen come to Christ during the week is an indescribable experience, one that changes you forever.

In January 2004 we were in Uganda on one of these mission trips. We were teaching pastors and church leaders in the mornings and then traveling about two hours to a village that did not have a church in it but wanted one. About twenty pastors would go with us each afternoon. We would go out in groups of three or four and visit homes praying with people and sharing the gospel of Jesus Christ with the people. We would conclude our visiting about 4:00 p.m. with an evangelistic service and then return to our "camp." At the end of the week we were planning to "open up a new church" in that village. That week I had an experience that has changed my vision for ministry.

I was teaching the pastors about how Jesus is our model as pastors; He is the Good Shepherd. We were looking at passages of Scripture in John 10, Ezekiel 34, and Matthew 25 on how Jesus feeds, leads, and cares for His sheep. I shared with the pastors from the parable that Jesus told in Matthew 25 of the King and how one day He will separate the sheep from the goats (parts of this are from Ezekiel 34). Jesus said that on that day He will say to the sheep, "I was hungry and you gave me something to eat. I was thirsty and you gave me something to drink … they will say, when did we ever see you hungry and give you to eat, or thirsty and give you something to drink? The King will say, whenever you did it to the least of these my brethren, you did it to me." The point that I was making was that when we give we do not give to need, we give to the King who is always closely identified with needs, and when we give, we give to Him as we give to needy people. Hold that point.

The village that we were traveling out to was right beside a huge prison. Prison conditions in Uganda are unspeakable. Families must provide food and soap and other necessities for their loved ones in prison or their loved ones will go wanting. These villages around the prisons are filled with these families and the needs are overwhelming. Alcohol is a serious problem all over the world but especially in these villages. The pastors wanted to see a church in this particular village so that a prison ministry could begin from the new church to the families of the prisoners and to the prisoners themselves.

The first afternoon we were in this village I noticed a little blind orphan boy about eight or nine years old. There are many orphans in Uganda because of the AIDS epidemic and you can spot the orphans by the ragged clothes that they wear. This little boy really got to me. One eye was completely gone and the other one was badly infected and swollen outside of the eye socket and eyelid. It was so horrible I could not even stand to look at him, but I was praying for him. I noticed him again during the worship service but had to turn my head away because he looked so bad.

During the invitation as many people were coming to Christ and the pastors were singing and counseling the new believers, I saw this boy standing there in the middle of everyone clapping with the music and I heard in my heart the Lord say, "go over and put your hands on the little boy's head and pray for him." I hesitated and answered back that it would scare the little boy if I did that because there was singing and clapping and people moving all around and talking and I did not have an interpreter. The Lord said, "You will be talking to Me, I do not need an interpreter, go over and put your hands on the little boy's head and pray for him."

I knew what I needed to do so I did. I noticed that when I put my hands gently on his head he froze with his little hands literally in mid-clap. I looked heaven-ward (mainly because I just could not look at the poor little boy because of that one horrible eye) and began to pray for his healing and care. As I prayed I was overwhelmed with joy like I had not experienced before. I did not know if it was because of all the people being saved or the pastors singing or what, but I got happy while praying for this little boy. I got to thinking that maybe God was healing the boy while I prayed and fully expected to look down and see new eyes! But when I looked down, there was that swollen-out-of-the-socket eye, but there was also a faint smile.

The next few days I did not see the boy but I was praying for him. I felt that God had placed this boy on my heart and had encouraged me to pray for him with that rush of joy that I had experienced when I prayed for him the first time. On Saturday we told everyone that we would be back the next day to start the new church. One of the new believers that lived right in the middle of the village made her home available for the new church to meet in until we could purchase the land and build a new building.

Sunday morning there were about forty people waiting for us and about another twenty arrived after we began singing. The little blind orphan boy was one of them. During the invitation several more received Christ. The new pastor was getting all of their names when the Lord spoke to me again, "See the little blind boy?" "Yes." "Pray for him again and this time anoint his eyes with oil. Use the eye ointment you have in the first aid kit." I protested. "Lord, I am not a doctor. I did not bring any gloves. I cannot touch that eye. I cannot even look at it. It might pop or something. I could do serious damage," (I realized this excuse must have been funny because that eye was as about as seriously damaged as an eye can get). I made several other excuses but it was undeniable what the Lord told me to do and I remembered how I had been teaching the pastors all week how important it is to be obedient to the Lord.

So I asked the interpreter to ask if the boy had any relatives around. A young man stepped forward and said that he was his cousin and that he was indeed an orphan. His parents had died from the AIDS epidemic. I told him to watch me and do what I was about to do everyday until the ointment was all gone. Then I told the interpreter to explain to the little boy what I was about to do, that I was going to pray for him and then put some medicine in his eyes. I think that I was praying more for myself than I was the boy. I said a prayer for him and then got the ointment ready. Then I prayed for myself asking God to help me do this.

The first eye (or rather eye cavity) was easy because there was not anything there, but I could see that other one out of the corner of my eye. I put some of the ointment on my finger, prayed, and anointed the cavity with the ointment. That was the easy one. The hard one was next. I prayed, "God, help me with this bad eye." When I looked at it I noticed that it had rolled up so that I did not have to look at the gross part. I was thankful for that and told God so, and then began to gently put the eye salve in praying that God would heal him. Again, I fully believed that we were all about to see new eyes appear, when suddenly the Lord spoke again, *"You just put ointment in My eyes!"* and I remembered the parable from Matthew 25, "… I was hungry and you gave Me something to eat … when did we ever see You hungry and give You something to eat … whenever you did it to the least of these My brethren you did it to Me." It hit me like a ton of bricks! Suddenly, my eyes were opened and I realized that *I was looking into the face of Jesus!*

In a split second all of the grossness and my reluctance were gone and I began to put more and more and more ointment in his eye with prayers of joy and thanksgiving that the Lord had allowed me to minister to Him by praying for the little orphan boy! *Ministry was transformed into an act of joyful, exuberant worship!*

Our view of the way things are is seriously limited by our tendency to forget that we are all primarily spiritual beings, made in the image of God, and that there is more to this life than just this life. God is infinite in every category, most of which we are not even aware of. He is love, He is light, He is always present, and He is more merciful, powerful, and wise than we can ever know. His plan for our lives is that we become like His Son, Jesus Christ, in every area of our lives. He is doing that good work in us continually by His Spirit who dwells in us.

His ways are not our ways and we must learn His ways. One of His ways is that when we help others we are helping Him. He is so closely identified with people who are in need, that when we help them, we worship Him. Serving others becomes worship when God opens our eyes to see how close He is to the hurting, the suffering, the lonely, and the oppressed, who are made in His image. When this transformation happens in our lives, joy enters the picture; ministry becomes an overflow of extravagant worship! We experience Christ with them and they experience Jesus Christ in us, and He is glorified by it all!

It was later as I reflected upon this experience more and continued to pray for little Waisawa, that is his name, which means "the twin" also hit me; I saw in his face the face of Jesus. Next time you are helping someone who is hurting, remember what Jesus said, "when you gave unto the least of these you gave to Me," and if you are praying for blind eyes to open, don't be surprised if the ones that get opened are yours!

Pastor's Prayer Partners

I was called as pastor of the First Baptist Church in Boerne, Texas in 1992. One Sunday morning, shortly after we arrived, a boy named Mason Finley came up to me after the worship service and said, "I am your prayer partner, Bubba. I pray for you before I come to church and always at night before bedtime." I was so moved by this young man and his prayers that before long I had asked other children if they wanted to be my prayer partners.

First, I would write their parents asking permission to write their child explaining the prayer partner ministry. Then, I would write to their child asking them if they were willing to be my prayer partner for the year. As my prayer partner they would pray for me and a few prayer requests that I would send them, and I would pray for them. When they would agree I would send them a "praying hands" pin and they became official pastor's prayer partners.

The first year we had about seventy-five children, ages six through 12 sign up. Part of being a prayer partner was agreeing to go on prayer-walking mission trips with me. Once a year all of the prayer partners would go to city hall, the police station, and the school district office, prayer-walk around it, then go inside, meet with the major, chief of police, and the school superintendent and then we would all go back to the church and have pizza together.

Later in the year we would take the older prayer partners, third through sixth graders to our state capitol in Austin for the day. Again, we would prayer-walk the capitol building, meet with our state senators and representatives, and others we had made appointments with. Once we got to go into the governor's office and prayed with his assistant. Of course, we would take several parents with us and everyone had to go through some missionary training classes before they could go. The church treated us just like any missionary being sent out by the church with financial support for some of our expenses and prayer support for each person.

And then, once a year, in the summer, we would take the sixth graders to Washington, D.C. for a week of prayer-walking. We would make appointments with our senators and representatives, and always with the president although we never met personally with him. We would get to prayer-walk his house with the other tour groups. We would prayer-walk the Capitol, the Supreme Court building, and Arlington National Cemetery. The students were required to complete several assignments before they could go. While in Washington, we would dress like we were going to meet with the president but with tennis shoes because we did so much walking. The following stories are of some of the experiences we had on some of those prayer-walking mission trips.

The second year we took sixth graders to Washington was the first time we prayer-walked the Supreme Court building. They were very strict inside the building. We walked along with all of the others on the tour and were careful not to break any of the rules. Once we got outside, on the steps, we all got together to pray. There were about fourteen students and about five adults. We shared together first about being in the building where so many of our laws are upheld and decided upon and decided to pray together before going on to the Capitol. I asked a girl and a boy to lead in the prayer. Like most of our prayer times in these public places, we did not close our eyes but kept them open. This is one of the first rules of prayer-walking!

As we were finishing up our prayer, a security guard came up to us and sternly told us to move off of the steps and to cross the street. "No demonstrations are allowed on the Supreme Court steps!" We apologized and began to move to the street. I noticed that one of our adults, an attorney, had stayed to talk with the guard. We crossed the street and were a bit on edge. One of our students said, "Cool, we almost got arrested for praying. We could have been like the apostle Paul and written letters to our parents from prison."

When our attorney sponsor crossed the street he informed us that this is one of the laws and that they watch with cameras very closely to see anything that resembles a demonstration. Apparently, we had resembled a demonstration although it was very low key what we were doing. One of the students said, "Jesus said that we are the light of the world and that a city on a hill cannot be hidden. Our light was shining too bright." Someone else said, "Prayer gets people's attention." Another said, "Wow, I never knew prayer to be so dangerous and powerful!"

One of the exciting experiences for many of the students on these prayer-walking mission trips was to ride the subway, called the Metro in Washington. For most of the students it was their first experience on a subway. We trained the students to pray for people who were getting on and off, and to stay together. By the end of the week they would be old hands at riding the subway. One of the most amazing things happened on the subway one year that we did not hear about until a few weeks after we returned home.

After we returned home that year an older sister of one of the students went to Washington to visit her aunt. Her aunt told her that one of the ladies at work had recently started asking her many questions about Christianity and especially about prayer. She was encouraged because this particular lady had been through several difficult experiences and had recently had a new look of hope and peace about her.

The older sister related this story to us after she returned from Washington. She said that her aunt's friend had said that it was so strange on a particular morning that she got on the Metro. She was feeling so depressed, as usual, and was simply going through the motions as she had for so many years. But on this morning she happened to see some nicely dressed students on the Metro standing beside her. One of them, a young lady, looked up at her and smiled and said, "I am going to pray for you today." The young lady then reached into her bag and handed her a booklet on prayer and said, "May God bless you as you read this today."

When the friend of the aunt arrived at work she was so excited to share how some students on the subway had encouraged her and how one of them even said that she was going to pray for her that day! The aunt said that she was a new person from that day on and had begun asking many questions and had even bought a Bible. As her aunt was sharing this, the older sister said, "That was my sister's prayer-walking group!" We assembled the students together after hearing about this and sure enough, one of our students remembered giving a lady one of the booklets on prayer and prayed for her. We never know the impact of a simple prayer and encouraging word.

The summer of 2001 was one of the most meaningful trips for all of us. It was just like the others in that we rode the Metro, prayer-walked through the White House as we walked through with the tour group, through the Capitol building and in the offices of our representatives, through the Supreme Court building, and Arlington. It was what happened after we came home that shook all of us to the very core; September 11, 2001.

Those were some of the most difficult days for everyone. We had prayer services every night for over a week. At each service we had times of sharing before we prayed. We experienced the full range of our emotions and grief. During one of those prayer services a group of students who had been in Washington only a few months before came to the microphone and shared with the congregation.

They said that they had heard that the plane that crashed into the Pentagon was suppose to crash into the White House but could not see it. And that the plane that crashed in Pennsylvania would have probably crashed into the Capitol. Then they stunned us all by saying that they believed that God had used them in prayer-walking to protect those buildings from disaster and they were grateful that God had used them that way.

We must never underestimate the power and influence of prayer, especially from someone who has the faith of a child.

"Jesus, and that's my final answer!"

I was the pastor of the First Baptist Church in Boerne for twelve years from 1992 until 2004. It was the best twelve years of my life. We loved the people and the people loved us, and we all grew together in that environment of love. It was very rewarding and fulfilling to be with people over the various stages of their lives.

We were with couples when they got married. We were with them when their children were born, and then got to pray for those children their first Sunday at church. I was able to visit with those children six or seven years later about being saved, and baptized them. We counseled teens as they decided on what college they would attend, saw them off to school, and then counseled them again about getting married and starting careers. We helped couples with aging parents, and waited with families in hospital waiting rooms. We limped through the deep waters of grief when the funerals were planned, and prayers were said at the cemetery. There were times when a wedding would be done, followed by a funeral, followed by a birth at the hospital, followed by a Sunday School class party, sometimes all on the same day. Deep relationships are developed in that setting, relationships that last forever because they revolve around and in Jesus Christ.

One of those relationships was with Bud and Ruth. Both were retired and yet very active in the life of the church, Ruth more so than Bud for health reasons. Bud had served in World War II as a fighter pilot. He was shot down twice, captured by the Germans, escaped, and lived to tell about it. As a POW, he and several others were being marched outside of the compound to be executed. He and a friend decided they would run for it. His friend was killed, but Bud managed to only be hit in the leg and was able to elude his captors. His leg got infected and he passed out, only to awake in a Gypsy camp. The Gypsies were ready to sell him to the first ones to come along willing to buy him. Luckily, General Patton and the Third Army were the first ones to come along. General Patton bought Bud for $25. This, of course, was the short version, the long version being much more detailed and exciting.

Ruth worked in the nursery, singing and sharing God's love with the three and four year-olds. She witnessed everywhere she went. She always talked about Jesus Christ and how He had changed her life. When she and Bud went to the bank to buy their first house as a young couple, so excited about the opportunity to own their home, they learned from the banker that they did not qualify because they gave so much to the church. The banker asked about their large contributions, and they told him that it was called tithing, giving 10% to the Lord in worship and with gratitude for all that God had given to them. The banker said that if they would simply cut back on giving so much then they would qualify for the loan.

Ruth said she felt like they would be denying their faith in Christ if they even considered such a thing. She spoke up and shared how much Jesus had done for them and given to them and they would not even think about it and would not be borrowing any money from him. But the conversation shifted to the banker and his relationship with Jesus Christ. Before they left, Ruth had led the banker to Christ and had his word that he would begin attending church. Ruth said, "We did not get to buy the house; we got something better than that; we got to see that banker come to church, get baptized, and bring his whole family to Christ!"

Bud's health declined and he died and went home to heaven to be with his Savior, Jesus Christ. We were all concerned about Ruth because Bud had taken such careful and close care of Ruth. Ruth went to work at Wal-Mart, first as greeter, then in the men's wear, then as floor manager of men's shirts. Ruth had found her place. She could witness freely and did. She could order the T-shirts with any logo she wanted; of course, most were about Jesus. And she advertised her merchandise by wearing the latest ones. She had shirts that said, "Got Jesus?" One of her favorites was from a game show of that time which said, "Jesus, and that's my final answer!" Ruth would always tell me about her most recent orders and how wonderful it was to work in a place that allowed such freedom.

Ruth remarried sometime later to a wonderful man named Bill who had known her for a long time. She continued her work at Wal-Mart, and Bill mowed lawns for people in the neighborhood and for church members. He called it his yard-mowing ministry. They were perfect for each other.

Then the unbelievable happened. Ruth went in for some simple medical tests, and cancer was discovered. It wasn't the bad kind she said, and no one was to worry. She would have to go through the chemo and radiation but said she never did like her hair anyway. When we would have prayer time during our worship services for the sick, Ruth would make her way down the aisle, not to be prayed for, but to pray for others. It was so moving to see Ruth in one of her hats kneeling beside someone who had just discovered they had cancer or beside some family member of a sick relative, and praying for them. Of course we would all pray for Ruth, but like her, we were not worried, just waiting for her hair to grow back.

During the treatments, Bill and Ruth were often on the road going for her treatments and eating out a lot. They started their prayer ministry during those trips. As they ordered their food they would tell the servers that they always prayed before they ate, and they would ask if the server had any prayer requests. This became an exciting ministry for Ruth. She told me she could not eat but loved meeting these nice people, hearing their prayer requests, and praying for them.

Bill and Ruth would always put a large tip in a tract and let the servers know they would be remembering their special requests in their prayers. At prayer meeting each Wednesday night, whenever they were back in town, they would share their long list of prayer requests from servers all across the country. They would make it a point to return to the same restaurants, ask for certain servers, inquire about how they were doing, and often pray with their new friends.

Ruth got worse and worse and some of us started worrying, but not Ruth. She told me one Sunday, "I am glorifying God in this situation, and I want people to see how a Christian suffers; with joy, gratitude, and hope." Ruth began to talk about heaven and how there was more to this life than just this life. Finally, she was not able to come to church anymore. Her three and four year-old Sunday School students would send her cards and the church family would go by and see her during those difficult and last days of her life. She would always talk about Jesus, even when she was not sure what she was saying because of the medication for the pain. Early one morning Bill called me and told me that Ruth had just graduated and that it was a glorious graduation.

At the funeral, many of Ruth's co-workers shared testimonies of how Ruth was always so joyful, grateful, and Christ-like. Some even shared how they had come to know Jesus Christ in a more personal way because of Ruth's encouragement and witness. Church members whom

Ruth had prayed for and restaurant workers all talked about how Ruth had ministered to them.

On the way out to the cemetery, the funeral home director told me something that made me cry, as it does now while I write. He said that when Bill called the night she died, he went to their home and into the bedroom where Ruth's body was. He said there was a peace in the room that was unmistakable and when he saw Ruth's body he knew why. She was wearing one of her old Wal-Mart shirts, the one that said in big, bold letters,

"Jesus, and that's my final answer!"

I could not end Ruth's story without sharing one more thing. God created us in His image and gave us a perfect relationship with Himself. But the first chance we had, we sinned, and the relationship died. The Bible says that all have sinned and fallen short of the glory of God, and the wages of sin is death (Romans 3:23, 6:23).

But God would not leave us in that hopeless condition. He loved us and gave His only begotten Son for us so that we would not perish but have eternal life (John 3:16). God sent Jesus to live the life that He created us to live and then Jesus gave us His life on the cross to pay the penalty for our sins, something we could never do on our own.

On the third day, God raised Jesus from the dead and gave Him the Name above all names so that we could be saved. When we call upon that Name, the Lord Jesus Christ, and by faith repent of our sins and commit our lives to Him, we are saved (Romans 10:9-13). We are saved from the wrath of God and are given a new relationship with God; an eternal relationship with Jesus Christ and a new identity in Him. By faith in Christ we are now children of God and joint heirs with Christ (Galatians 3:26).

This new relationship with God by faith in Jesus Christ begins with a prayer of faith. Would you like to pray that prayer right now? You can if you are willing to begin a new relationship with God. Pray this prayer and make these words your own;

"Lord Jesus Christ, I am a sinner and I need to be saved. Save me Lord Jesus, by your sinless life and your death on the cross and give me the new relationship with God by your resurrection from the dead. I repent of my sin and ask you into my heart to be my Savior and Lord of my life. Live your life as me in the world for I now desire to glorify God. Thank You, Lord Jesus. In the Name above every name I pray; In the Name of Jesus Christ. AMEN."

If you prayed that prayer you have been born again and now have a new relationship with God by faith in Jesus Christ. Find a church to share this commitment with and begin reading and studying God's Word. God will give you spiritual growth as you follow Jesus Christ in worship, Bible study, fellowship with God's people, and serving Christ by helping others. God will teach you to live now the way we will live in heaven; loving Him and others with Him.

When Jesus Christ comes back again, as He promised He would, we will join Him and all those who have gone before us and we will all share our stories together and say;

"Not unto us, O LORD, not unto us, but to your Name give glory, because of your steadfast love and your faithfulness."

Endnotes

1. "Scripture quotations are from The Holy Bible, English Standard Version, copyright 2001 by Crossway Bibles, a publishing ministry of Good News Publishers.

A Vision of the Beautiful Bride of Jesus Christ

Ephesians 5:25-27
Preached at the First Baptist Church in Corpus Christi, TX
August 12, 2007
By Bubba Stahl, pastor

This passage of Scripture is often used to describe how husbands and wives are to love each other and so reflect the reality of Jesus Christ and His love for His Body, the Church. The apostle Paul tells us that he is talking about a profound mystery, of Christ and His Church. We recognize a person when we see their head, their face. You cannot recognize a person by looking at their body, but rather at their head. There are those who do not know this and need to learn it. When you look at someone, look at their head for this is the most important feature of us all and the way we are recognized. And so it is for the Bride of Jesus Christ, the Church. She is a most beautiful bride and her most outstanding feature is her Head, Jesus Christ.

This beautiful Bride, the Church, has many other features that contribute to her beauty. She is lovely, and she loves her King. I first saw this beautiful Bride the morning after our (Beth and I) first interview with the pastor search committee of this church in 2004. We had met with the committee for several hours that evening and it did not go so well. I had done some research on the church (Dr. Elmore's history book of FBC-CC) and of the area and had several questions myself.

We spent the night at the ranch house of the chairman of the committee. I could not go to sleep that night because I kept thinking about the situation of the church and of some ideas that I had, but every idea that I had would just evaporate and then I would try to come up with some other solution. Around 3 in the morning I finally just gave up. I remember praying, "Lord, I do not know what this church needs, but I do know I do not have it. Send them someone who does. I'll talk to You in the morning. Give us a safe trip back to Boerne. AMEN." I felt a great burden lifted and a soft blanket of peace came over me and I went right to sleep.

The next morning I woke up early and was having coffee with John at his breakfast table. He was talking about something but I was thinking about the appointments that I had that afternoon in Boerne. Suddenly, in my heart, I could see a beautiful Bride kneeling down by the harbor bridge giving something to a Filipino seaman. I could see his face as he was receiving something from her but I could tell that he was receiving something much more than the thing she was giving; I could tell that he was receiving Jesus Christ. His face was lit up with joy and peace.

Immediately, I saw a long line of people from every segment of society in Corpus Christi receiving something from this lovely Bride; each one receiving Jesus Christ with the same look of joy and peace. I saw a single mom with children at her side, a teenager with a skate board, a business man in a nice suit, a business woman, a family, an elderly couple, a grieving man, a homeless lady, a Navy pilot, a university student, on and on, each one standing before this kneeling Bride receiving something and receiving Christ as they did.

Then the whole scene began to turn and I was able to see the face of this Bride. She was beautiful indeed. I cannot describe her face except to say that she was "come alive gorgeous!" As she knelt before all of these people, giving them various things to help them in their particular need, I could tell that she was looking at someone other than the person; she was looking into the face of her King! I remembered the words of Jesus in Matthew 25 when he said, "… I was hungry and you gave Me something to eat, I was thirsty and you gave Me something to drink.… When did we ever see You hungry and give You something to eat or thirsty and give You something to drink? Whenever you did it unto one of the least of these My brethren you did it unto Me." I saw that her ministry to others was an act of worship to her King and Lord, Jesus Christ. Wow, I had never had that thought before nor had I ever seen anything like that before.

Tears were beginning to roll down my face and John had stopped talking because he could tell I was not listening to him. It was a bit awkward to say the least, and in a short time Beth and I were on IH 37 heading back to Boerne. I shared with Beth what God had shown me and I knew that it was from Him and was what the Church in Corpus Christi needed to see and hear.

In a month or so the committee invited us to come back to the ranch house for a second interview. I do not remember very many of their questions that evening but I do remember sharing the vision of the beautiful bride with much excitement. I think my excitement may have caused some concern among them and it was a bit bold but I had seen it so clearly, that beautiful kneeling Bride giving and sharing Christ. I did not hear back from them for a couple of months. It was after the third interview that God made it clear to them and to us that He was sending us from First Baptist Church in Boerne to First Baptist Church in Corpus Christi.

We headed back to Boerne on a Wednesday morning with a great deal of excitement because God had made it so clear and yet I was not looking forward to the next few days back in Boerne. That afternoon I called the staff together in Boerne and shared the vision with them. It was a hard time. No one had any idea of the interviews we had been having. Up until the last interview I was still wondering if God was maybe just testing us, like Abraham when God told him to sacrifice Isaac, to see if we loved Him more than the blessings He had given to us in Boerne. But after that last interview it was crystal clear that He was sending us to Corpus Christi, which meant that we had to say good-bye to people that we had grown to love over a 12-year pastorate in Boerne.

On Saturday, I called the leadership of the Church together and shared the vision with them, and then on Sunday with the whole Church. While I was sharing with the Church in Boerne why we were leaving the chairman of the search committee here was sharing that we were coming in view of call to be the next pastor of First Baptist Church in Corpus Christi. In a few weeks we were back in Corpus Christi and I shared the vision of the beautiful Bride with this Church for the first time. The first time I met with our staff I shared this vision. For the past three years I have looked at that Bride over and over and asking God, "What is it that is so beautiful about her?" But for the past three years all I have been able to see was that kneeling Bride giving to all of those people, worshipping her King as she gave.

Around March of this year I began to get a bit discouraged. There were several factors that were contributing to this discouragement, but mostly I was thirsty, for water, I think. Maybe it was a spiritual thirst as well, but I do know that I was borderline dehydrated. My voice began to give-out, and dry-out, and I was tired all the time, even in the mornings. Beth and I had already planned to spend Father's Day weekend with our two sons and their families in San Antonio and the week before Father's Day I asked for a week of sick leave, two weeks of vacation, and a week of conference time off. The church graciously gave me these four weeks to be away and recover.

The first week I drank gallons of water and immediately started feeling better. By the end of the second week I had stopped thinking about what I needed to say on Sunday. And by the end of the third week I was feeling back to normal. During this time I was also beginning to see this beautiful bride in **high definition**. The last week of my time off, Beth and I went to Lebh Shomea, the House of Prayer silent monastery on the Kenedy Ranch. I have been going there over the past three years for one and two-day silent prayer retreats. We were able to stay six days. During those days of silence and solitude and prayer God brought this beautiful Bride up close for me to see in greater detail. I was able to see her breath; she breathes the Holy Spirit. And I saw four beautiful features in the DNA of the Bride. God showed me *a church of small groups, each one led by the Holy Spirit and four people: a prayer warrior, a servant-hearted missionary, a true worshipper, and a Bible teacher.*

When I say "small groups" I mean Sunday School classes, prayer groups, and/or weekday Bible study groups. Some of these classes meet on Sunday morning, some on Sunday night, some on Monday morning, some on Tuesday morning, some are for women, others for men, some are strictly for children or students, others are for couples. One thing that they all have in common is that they pray and study God's Word together. I have been able to count about 56 of these classes from our first grade Sunday School class on up. These 56 classes have about 650 in weekly attendance.

I see these four core leaders in each small group recruiting people from their small group in the prayer ministry, missions ministry, worship ministry, and Bible-learning ministry of the whole Church. For example, the prayer warrior can encourage the small group to send two or three pray-ers into our prayer room each week. Presently we have about 30 prayer warriors in our prayer room each week. Just think, if each of our 56 small groups would send just two from their group within a few months we could see over 100 people personally involved in the prayer room ministry; and I do see it!

And I see each small group adopting another small group in the church, and praying for them. I also see each small group adopting another church in our area, a school, and an area of our city to pray for. They will pray for missionaries that we send out weekly, monthly, and annually into the harvest. Obviously, we cannot pray for all of those concerns each time, but we can pray for one of them each time and in a short time cover them all. The prayer warrior of each small group can keep these prayer concerns before the group each time they meet and recruit for the prayer ministry from their own small group.

The servant-hearted missionary would do the same, but in the area of missions. We presently have about 250 different people serving as missionaries in about 54 areas of missions locally, in our state, nation, and world. Most of these mission projects are local, many of them right here at our church. A missionary is someone who is sent to help someone else with something. Jesus said it may only be a cup of cold water, but even that requires someone who is willing to go and share it with someone who is thirsty. But God is the One who sends us out with something to share in the Name of His Son, Jesus Christ. When we do, no matter what it is or how it is received, He is glorified.

I see the missionary in each small group recruiting missionaries from his or her group and sending them out into the local, regional, national, and ends-of-the-earth mission fields. Not everyone in the group can go, but most can and will. I see these missionaries going over to the Recreation Center each week to help with all of the needs in our recreation ministry. I see missionaries from our small groups going over to the

Way Inn each week and serving people food (Jesus said, "I was hungry and you gave Me something to eat."). I can see our small groups sending missionaries down to the kitchen on Wednesdays for our evening meal and on Thursday afternoons to prepare the sandwiches that the Thursday night street ministry missionaries will hand out on the streets. I see each small group sending out missionaries to all of the growing ministry opportunities that God is bringing to us. Some of these small group missionaries will go to Uganda, some to China, some to Austria, some to the Dominican Republic, some to Haiti, and some to Mexico. Others will be sent out from our groups to our annual mission trip to New York City.

One of the new mission trips we are planning is to our own city, Corpus Christi, each month on a Saturday. We are asking God to send out, two-by-two, prayer-walking missionaries to the university campus, to the bay front, to the downtown area, to the parks, and on the bus lines (prayer-riding missionaries). All of these places are places where people gather and are in need of prayer. I see these prayer-walking missionaries praying on these sites ready to share a good word for the Lord and ready to hear prayer requests (which they can call back to our prayer room that day). In doing this we will be praying for Corpus Christi by praying with the people of Corpus Christ. I see many people getting saved in these Saturday mission trips to our own city.

The servant-hearted missionary will keep these mission opportunities before the small group and will encourage his or her small group to be personally involved in missions because the message we share is a personal message of a personal relationship with God through faith in Jesus Christ. The missionaries of our church will multiply because each small group will have a servant-hearted missionary encouraging everyone in the small group to be involved. And each one of our missionaries will be covered in prayer by the prayer warriors of each small group. This is called unity in the body.

Each small group that meets on Sunday morning, Sunday night, Monday night, Tuesday morning, and all during the week will, each time they meet, worship and adore Jesus Christ because every small group will have a true worshipper in it. What is a true worshipper? Is this someone with a singing voice? Well, maybe, or maybe not. I can't sing but I can worship. In fact, every believer can worship because in Christ we all have the same Spirit, the Holy Spirit, and He loves to glorify and exalt the Lord Jesus Christ! A true worshipper is one who worships God in Spirit and in truth. This is who God is looking for. Our Abba is not looking for praise and worship, He is looking for worshippers who will praise Him from the heart. He created us for this. He is seen by His own creation when we give Him praise.

I see every small group taking time during the time they are together to focus their attention and affection on Jesus Christ. This can be done in many different ways. Certainly, worship can be given by the small group singing a beautiful song of praise. Or maybe the true worshipper will lead the group in a Psalm of praise from God's Word. He or she may lead the group in a time of "look at this ..." prayer, vividly describing Jesus Christ from one of the many word pictures of Him in the Bible while everyone is in a spirit of prayer. The true worshipper will turn and tune the small group's attention and affection toward desiring the presence of Jesus Christ in their midst.

I can see our small groups developing worship teams and joining with other small groups and their worship teams and having a "praise fest" where Jesus Christ is enjoyed by all and all enjoy fellowship with Him and with each other (and of course some good food, too!). I see these worship teams getting together at the church during the week and praising God in our Chapel or Sanctuary. This is beautiful to our Lord as we sing and speak His Name and praises. I can hear this sound as it is amplified out into the hallways, sidewalks, and parking lots of our church so that as soon as a person steps out of their car they begin hearing the high praises of our King!

Of course, we will not want to have it so loud as to disturb our neighbors, but rather to encourage people who come to church during the week as we listen in on what God is listening to from our praise teams. The Bible states that from the rising of the sun to the setting of the same the Name of the LORD is to be praised. I see and hear that happening through our small group true worshipper and the praise that will come from every small group.

All 56 of our present small groups have a Bible teacher in them. We will continue to see the Bible being taught as our small groups begin to multiply. We need to be taught the eternal truth from God's Word and be encouraged and instructed to apply that truth to our lives regularly. Discovering the life-transforming truth of the Bible together with others in a small group is the place where God gives us spiritual growth. I see our Bible teachers in every small group being trained by the best Bible teachers in the area.

We are just a few miles from the South Texas School of Christian Studies. I see us working together with them to develop a training course for our Bible teachers that if they choose to, they may receive college and seminary credit. We have a good relationship with the administration and faculty of this school. We will begin shortly to discover how we can partner for this kind of seminary level continuous education. I see us making this available for every small group Bible teacher; not mandatory, but made available at our church campus.

I see this beautiful Bride of Jesus Christ, a church of small groups, led by the Holy Spirit and four people; a prayer warrior, a servant-hearted missionary, a true worshipper, and a Bible teacher, developing rapidly and growing exponentially over the next 10 years. I believe that we are in for a three-fold doubling over the next 10 years; a decade of abundance! We presently have 56 small groups. I see us having 100 within two years, and then doubling again within five years to 200, then doubling again over the next five years. I see a beautiful Bride of 400 small groups, each one led by the Holy Spirit and four people by the year 2017.

I also see our prayer room doubling within a year to over 100 people filling fourteen hours a day (from 7am until 9pm) seven days a week. We will not stop there; I see us opening up another prayer room and continuing to provide a place for our prayer warriors coming out of our small groups to pray; then another, then another. I see us having four prayer rooms, one on the south side of the building, one on the north, the east, and the west, all filled from 7am until 9pm with intercessors from our small groups crying out to God on behalf of others. Wow! Think of it!

I see a whole army of missionaries, over 2,000 a year, going out and coming back weekly, monthly, and annually to our Jerusalem, Judea, Samaria, and to the ends of the earth, sharing with others the unsearchable riches of Christ through evangelism, construction, medical/dental, teaching, prayer-walking, and encouraging projects; each one with a team of intercessors praying for them while they are serving and rejoicing with them when they return. Every small group will be able to hear from their missionaries what they saw God do. "Only You can make it happen, Lord, so make it happen, God!"

I can hear our worship teams, all from our small groups, singing and speaking praises to God throughout the week in our small groups and on the church property. I can see our Bible teachers learning, hungry to receive so that they can give to their small groups the rich treasures from God's Word. And no one is left out because everyone can pray, be personally involved in missions, worship, and learn the Bible. I see all of the small groups gathering together every weekend in our sanctuary in four or five worship settings and celebrating together the goodness and beauty of our King! How good He is! And oh, how beautiful!

Another thing I see is a radical change in our budget. We have just received our new budget plan for 2007/2008. In our new budget we will spend 80% on personnel and building maintenance, and 20% on missions and ministries. By 2017 I see our budget reflecting the opposite; by then we will see 80% being given to missions and ministries and 20% on personnel and building maintenance. "Only You can make it happen, Lord, so make it happen, God!" One of the most beautiful features of this vision is that it does not require a rapidly expanding building or staff; it requires the Holy Spirit and four people in every small group leading them in prayer, missions, worship, and Bible learning. But of all of the beauty of the Bride, her most outstanding feature is her Head, Jesus Christ. He is the One who will be seen and heard by the watching world. They have seen enough of us. What the world needs to see and hear is Jesus Christ.

There are many questions that have been raised since I preached this message last Sunday. This has stimulated much conversation to say the least! How can we be sure? How could this be? What will it mean? These are only a few of the many questions. But let's remember to keep our focus on Jesus Christ. The question I have for you is this; as you heard it last Sunday and while you read it now, did something move within you? Was there a stirring in your heart? I know there was; but do you know what it was? I can tell you that I believe it was the Holy Spirit saying to you, "Only I can make it happen; and it will bring out the Lord Jesus Christ to the watching world in high definition; so ask and prepare for it; it's coming!"

I shared last Sunday, August 12, that I had been preparing this sermon for the past 25 years. On Monday morning Beth told me that I would spend the next 25 years explaining it and we agreed together that we would also be able to watch God do it right before our eyes, and we prayed, "Only You can make it happen, Lord, so make it happen, God!" Let's pray that prayer together and begin moving together in this direction. We will take one step at a time, together. We are not in a hurry but we are moving forward, together, with prayer, and a desire that this will reveal to the watching world how awesome is our King!

Stay tuned; to the Holy Spirit!

Bibliography

The Holy Bible, English Standard Version. Copyright 2001 by Crossway Bibles, Wheaton, Illinois: Good News Publishing, 2001.

978-0-595-46627-6
0-595-46627-3

CPSIA information can be obtained
at www.ICGtesting.com
Printed in the USA
FFHW021806060819
54127206-59821FF